Joanna Lumley

GW00459084

# Strands of History

# Strands of History

*Northbank Revealed*

by Clive Aslet

First published in 2014 by Wild Research,
40 Great Smith Street, London SW1P 3BU

**www.wildsearch.org**

© Wild Research 2014

© Text Clive Aslet 2014

All rights reserved

The Northbank BID
West Wing, Somerset House,
Strand, London WC2R 1LA

**www.thenorthbank.org**

ISBN 978-0-9576966-2-4

Printed by
OZGraf Olsztyńskie Zakłady Graficzne S.A.
ul. Towarowa 2, 10-417 Olsztyn, Poland

'Looking to Northumberland House, and turning your back upon Trafalgar Square, the Strand is perhaps the finest street in Europe, blending the architecture of many periods; and its river ways are a peculiar feature and rich with associations.'

Benjamin Disraeli, *Tancred: or, The New Crusade*, 1847

'I often shed tears in the motley Strand for fullness of joy at so much life... Have I not enough, without your mountains?'

Charles Lamb, turning down an invitation from William Wordsworth to visit him in the Lake District

# Contents

# About the Author

Clive Aslet is an award-winning writer and journalist, acknowledged as a leading authority on Britain and its way of life. In 1977 he joined the magazine *Country Life*, was for thirteen years its Editor and is now Editor at Large. He writes extensively for papers such as the *Daily Telegraph*, the *Daily Mail* and the *Spectator*, and often broadcasts on television and radio. He is well-known as a campaigner on the countryside and other issues. His novel, *The Birdcage*, was published in 2014.

# Foreword

## *The Lord Shuttleworth KCVO*

### *Chairman of the Council, Duchy of Lancaster*

In 2015, the Duchy of Lancaster will mark the 750th anniversary of the creation of the Lancaster Inheritance. Still owning the Savoy Estate between the Strand and the Embankment, the Duchy surely has a strong claim to be the longest inhabitant in the area of London now known as Northbank, the subject of this timely and fascinating book by Clive Aslet.

The Inheritance can be traced back to Peter of Savoy, whose niece, Eleanor of Aquitaine, wife of King Henry III, gave the manor of the Savoy to her second son, Edmund, Earl of Lancaster. It was Edmund's grandson who was created the first Duke of Lancaster, and the Inheritance passed to his daughter Blanche, who married John of Gaunt. It was in 1399 that Henry Bolingbroke, then Duke of Lancaster, claimed the crown of England and declared that his Lancaster inheritance should forevermore be held as a private estate of the monarch, separate from all other Crown lands. The Duchy remains to this day the owner of most of the site of John of Gaunt's immense Palace of the Savoy, notwithstanding its physical destruction by Wat Tyler and others during the Peasants' Revolt as long ago as 1381. One of our buildings, the enchanting Queen's Chapel of the Savoy, originally built in 1512 as part of the hospital created on the ruined site by Henry VII, may be the oldest building on the north bank of the Thames between Westminster Hall and Temple Church.

It is precisely because of our place in the history of the Northbank area that the Duchy of Lancaster will play its part, along with many neighbours, owners and occupiers, in the developing vision for its future. While safeguarding and indeed promoting the history and rich traditions of the area, its thoroughfares and buildings, we also want to participate in its evolutionary development. For example, we expect to continue our custom of beating the bounds of the manor of the Savoy, with members of the Council led on foot by the Clerk and the Chapel Steward and choir from one boundary marker to the next, set in the walls of various offices, a theatre, and the Embankment itself. At the same time, we are pleased that in addition to our mix of modern retail and office space, we have recently introduced some new student accommodation, recognising the increasing value of people living in Northbank.

I first came across the work of Clive Aslet some twenty-five years ago. When I was appointed chairman of a government agency, the Rural Development Commission, I asked a respected senior civil servant to recommend some background reading about relevant issues. He said there was not much available but I should have a look at some of the things written by 'young man called Aslet', who in his words 'seems to talk some sense'. Since then, Clive has produced much thoughtful and informed work as an author, a journalist, and a renowned editor of *Country Life*. With his expert eye for detail, and a strong sense of tradition and place, but with plenty of original ideas for the future, he is just the person to write about Northbank. With this book, Clive demonstrates a real feeling for the character of the area, and for its evolution as an important part of our capital city.

*Shuttleworth*
*August 2014*

# THE
# NORTHBANK

TRAFALGAR SQ · STRAND · ALDWYCH

Proposed area is subject to consultation

0    50    100 Metres

Reproduced from Ordnance Survey mapping with the sanction of Her Majesty's Stationery Office, Crown Copyright. City of Westminster LA100019597. J:\D_City Planning Group\H drive group data\Brooker Laurence\GIS 9.3

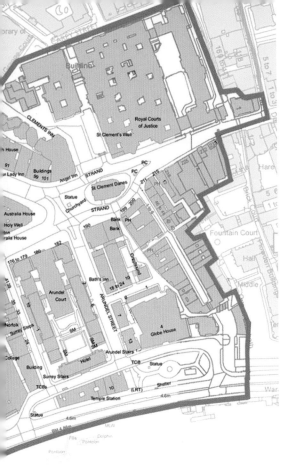

FIG 1

*Map of the Northbank Business Improvement District's 'footprint', stretching from Trafalgar Square in the west along the Strand and the Victoria Embankment as far as Aldwych and the Royal Courts of Justice in the east. Countless landmarks fall within the boundary.*

# Chapter One
## *The River*

First there was the river. It did not look like the modern Thames, corseted between nineteenth-century embankments. Two thousand years ago it resembled a piece of fraying cloth, broader and shallower than the present river, which wove its way between a mass of little islands. To either side was an ambiguous area, neither wholly river nor wholly land, made up of mudflats, reed beds and marshes. Herons fished here. So did communities who made their living from the river. A road grew up, going to the bridge built by the Romans. It ran along the steep-sided ridge that went parallel to the river. It came to be called simply 'Strand'.

To begin with, London was nothing more than the walled City of London, a square mile. Wealthy individuals had country estates outside the walls: evidence of one of them may survive in the so-called Roman Bath that exists in Strand Lane, an alley off Surrey Street. This 'fifteen-foot enigma' is, in its present form, largely Tudor, but the spring which feeds it bubbles into a Roman reservoir. A Roman coffin and pottery have also been found in the area. (The bath remained in use into the Victorian period, when Charles Dickens so much enjoyed his plunges that he wrote about them in *David Copperfield*; less happily, the antiquarian William Weddell, MP, died 'from a sudden chill' after plunging in, in 1792).

'To begin with, London was nothing more than the walled City of London, a square mile.'

It was not only the rich who congregated in these parts. The civic authorities excluded outsiders — undesirables of all description — from the comforts and protection of the City. Tanneries, gaols, brothels, play houses — anything that would upset the not-over-

FIG 2
The Thames from Somerset House Terrace towards the City, *by Canaletto, circa 1750, part of a pair of paintings by the Italian artist. Its counterpart looks along the river in the opposite direction towards Westminster.*

*When Canaletto painted this view, Somerset House was still much as it had been when rebuilt for Charles I's Widow Queen Henrietta Maria after the Restoration – 'mighty magnificent and costly,' according to Pepys. However, George III's Queen Charlotte preferred Buckingham House, and in 1774 large parts of Somerset House collapsed. The site was then cleared to make way for the present building.*

fastidious nostrils or moral sensibilities of the Middle Ages — could only settle down around the City's skirts. In an earlier period, Scandinavian settlers — the friendlier face, as one might hope, of the Viking migrations — were also kept at arm's length. Had they been fiercer, they would not, presumably, have been content with land west of the City, well-watered by streams flowing briskly towards the Thames, but otherwise somewhat lonely. As it was, they are remembered in the name of the church of St Clement Danes, its location perhaps originally related to the spring which fed the Roman baths.

St Clement was a Pope who died at the end of the first century when the Emperor Trajan ordered him to be tied to an anchor and thrown into the sea. He became the patron saint of sailors, as well as feltworkers, and as such had a special appeal to the seafaring Vikings, or those of them that were Christian. Danes had settled the area between the City of London and Westminster known as the Ald wic, or old village ('wic' being the Saxon equivalent of the Latin 'vicus', the smallest form of settlement recognised by the Romans; it seems to have been used by the Saxons to signify a village

near an old Roman fortification, in this case London). They may have taken over a small wooden church that already existed; if so, this was rebuilt in stone in the reign of the King Cnut (himself a Dane) at the beginning of the eleventh century. It was one of several churches with Scandinavian names, five in the City being dedicated to St Olaf (or Olave), the zealously Christian King Olaf Haraldsson of Norway who had been canonised after his death in battle in 1030. The impression given by a charter of 951, bestowed by King Edgar on the small Benedictine monastery that became Westminster Abbey, is that it was a bleak spot, referred to simply as London Fen. It sounds as though it would have been damp and marshy.

According to another source, however, the area a little to the west of St Clement Danes was 'a delightful spot, surrounded with fertile lands and green fields and near the main channel of the river, which bore abundant merchandise of wares of every kind for sale from the whole world to the town on its banks.' Here, 'hard by the famous and rich town of London,' Edward the Confessor established a royal palace on Thorney Island, an eyot isolated on the northern side by branches of the river Tyburn. Intensely pious, he also re-endowed and enlarged King Edgar's abbey, building a church in honour of St Peter. This became known as the 'west minster,' to distinguish it from the east minster of St Paul's Cathedral. Its importance was acknowledged when William I had himself crowned in Westminster Abbey, founding a tradition that has been continued with every coronation since. His son William Rufus rebuilt Westminster Hall as the largest covered structure north of the Alps. Communication between the court, from which England was ruled, and the City of London, its most important port and place of trade, was crucial. That link was made by Strand, which became — in terms of the prestige of the people who travelled it, and no doubt the value of goods they took with them — one of the most important thoroughfares in the country.

But for most of London's history it has been easier to travel by boat than over land. From Greenwich to Richmond, the great Tudor palaces, to which Henry VIII withdrew for fear of plague, could be reached by barge. Wherrymen plied a busy trade, even in the seventeenth century, bitterly objecting to the construction of the new bridges — Westminster, Waterloo — which destroyed their trade. Samuel Pepys habitually took their light, shallow craft,

whether to visit the dockyards at Deptford or merely to cross the river. Land that fronted the river was therefore desirable, and prelates, princes and a rich military order vied for space on the former marshes — drained by the early thirteenth century — between Blackfriars and Charing Cross. The Strand became a street of palaces which, in the exuberant opinion of one Edwardian writer, was 'not to be surpassed by any street in medieval Europe.'

# The Temple

The military order was the Knights Templar. They were an international order of warrior monks, founded in the decades after the First Crusade in order to protect pilgrims on their way to the newly recaptured city of Jerusalem. Distinguished by their white robes and tunics, emblazoned with the red cross that was the symbol of the Crusades, the Templars lived by the Rule of St Benedict, the standard monastic rule of the time, their day ordered by a round of devotions. Like other monks, the Templars were supposed to be celibate, and wore their hair short and even tonsured; their under garments, made of sheepskin, were never changed. But in contrast to these ascetic practices, they grew long beards, as facial hair was deemed to be a sign of masculinity to Moslems, and the

# Two Temple Place

The American millionaire William Waldorf Astor was an introverted, controlling, paranoid man. In London, he lived at Two Temple Place, which he also used as an estate office, boasting that every lock in the building could be shut at the touch of a central button. Not only did he install the largest strong room in Europe but two other enormous fortified safes. Apparently he feared being kidnapped; at Hever Castle, to which he moved after giving Cliveden to his son as a wedding present, he had the drawbridge pulled up after him at night. But whatever the fears that haunted him, he also had an impeccable eye for quality when it came to architecture. Two Temple Place is one of London's most charming buildings.

Even passers-by can appreciate the craftsmanship. Above the roof sails a gilded caravel: the Santa Maria in which Columbus discovered America. Before the front door stand two lamp standards, decorated with pairs of putti; as a salute to the technological advances of the age – work began in 1892 – one makes a telephone call, while the other demonstrates the triumph of electric light.

Inside, the floor of the hall is made of geometrical patterns of inlaid marble, called Cosmati work, inspired by the thirteenth-century pavement in front of the high altar of Westminster Abbey, where Astor's architect, John Loughborough Pearson, was surveyor. Progress up the great oak staircase is punctuated by figures from Astor's favourite book, *The Three Musketeers*. In the great hall on the first floor, a gilded frieze includes fifty-four characters from history and romance, linked by nothing except Astor's own imagination; among them are Pocahontas, Machiavelli, Bismarck, Anne Boleyn, and Marie Antoinette. Astor's fortune came from the United States, where Astor's forebear, John Jacob Astor, had made a fortune from fur-trapping in the late eighteenth century, then invested in farms on the edge of New York; this property became some of the most expensive real estate in the world. Born in 1848, William Waldorf Astor disliked his native land, where the press was intrusive and critical. After some years as American Minister in Rome, he moved to England in 1891, buying Cliveden, a house of ducal opulence overlooking the Thames. That was also Elizabethanised by Pearson. After Pearson's death, it was his son John Frank Pearson who built the new wing at Hever Castle – to which Astor moved after giving Cliveden to his son as a wedding present – in the form of a Tudor village.

The British lexicon does not have an equivalent of the French *Belle Epoque* or the American Gilded Age – couldn't one be invented to describe Astor's homes? Two Temple Place is now owned by the Bulldog Trust.

FIG 4
*Two Temple Place exterior.*

FIG 5
*Templar statue, courtyard of Temple church.*

*The Knights Templar were an international order of warrior monks, founded in the decades after the First Crusade in order to protect pilgrims on their way to the newly recaptured city of Jerusalem.*

Templars believed that their assertively hirsute faces would make them all the more terrifying. They carried swords, rode horses (up to three apiece) and were served by squires.

The Templars arrived in England in 1128, establishing themselves on a site in Holborn. That land was sold in 1161 and they moved to the river. In time, they would be joined by the Dominican friars of what became known as Blackfriars, while, to the north, lay pastures owned by the Convent (or Abbey) of St Peter, Westminster — now Covent Garden. The New Temple, as the Templars' new home was called, lay to the west of the river Fleet, one of the bigger streams flowing into the Thames. It had enough ground for military training and the exercise of horses. In 1185, the Patriarch of Jerusalem consecrated their church, in the presence of the King himself, Henry II. Like all Templar churches, it was round-nave, in homage to the Church of the Holy Sepulchre in Jerusalem. The character of some of the Templars' powerful supporters can be imagined from the effigies: they show heavily armed knights, some of whom are in the act of drawing their swords. The order even enjoyed the patronage of successive kings, to the extent that Henry III let it be known that he wished to be buried in the church. To this end, the Templars added a long choir, lined with black marble columns, in 1240 — though as it turned out, by the time of his death Henry III had decided to be buried in his rebuilt Westminster Abbey.

As the choir demonstrates, the austere and martial Templars had become rich. They were also independent, and felt able to stand up to mere kings, since their allegiance was directly to the Pope. This made them popular with wealthy magnates in need of a stronghold — safe even from light-fingered kings — in which to store gold and jewels. In time, it made them distinctly unpopular with kings, who feared they would become over-mighty. The reaction began in France: King Philip the Fair accused the Templars of heresy, a crime which conveniently allowed him to seize their assets, and in 1314 the last Grand Master, Jacques de Molay, was burned at the stake. The order had been abolished by the Pope seven years earlier. In England, Edward II took control of the London Temple, giving it eventually to the Order of St John: the fraternally rival Knights Hospitaller, whose gatehouse still survives in

> ‘The Templars were independent, and felt able to stand up to mere kings.’

Smithfield as the headquarters of the St John Ambulance Brigade.

The Knights Hospitaller rented the Templars’ exercise yard to two colleges of lawyers, who came to be called the Middle and Inner Temple. Henry VIII seized the lands of the Hospitallers, but James I confirmed the rights of the Middle and Inner Temple as two of London’s inns of courts. The Temple church was adopted as their own.

## Medieval, Tudor and Stuart Palaces

Today, half a millennium after the Thames palaces approached their zenith, little physical evidence of them remains. The only structure to hint at their former glory is the York Watergate, a work of Baroque exuberance by Nicholas Stone, dating from the 1620s. The Watergate provided a suitably magnificent entry for the Duke of Buckingham’s barge: now marooned in Embankment Gardens, a hundred and fifty yards inland from the Thames, it marks the point of the old river bank before the building of the Victoria Embankment in the 1860s.

If the cloud capp’d towers and gorgeous palaces have now faded, a memory of them survives in the street names. Medieval land usages determined the shape of later development.

In the eighteenth century, the poet John Gay evoked their vanished splendour:

*Behold that narrow street which steep descends,*
*Whose building to the slimy shore extends —*
*Here Arundel's fam'd structure rear'd its fame;*
*The street alone retains an empty name*
*Where Raphael's fair designs with judgment charm'd*
*Now hangs the bellman's song; and pasted here*
*The colour'd prints of Overton appear.*
*Where statues breathed, the works of Phidias' hands,*
*A wooden pump or lonely watch-house stands.*
*There Essex's stately pile adorn'd the shore;*
*There Cecil's, Bedford's, Villiers', now no more.*

Arundel House was one of the sights of London, not least because of the famous antiquities that were displayed there by its owner Thomas Howard, Earl of Arundel: 'to whose liberall charges and magnificence this angle of the world oweth the first sight of Greeke and Romane Statues,' as the scholar Henry Peacham put it in his *Compleat Gentleman* of 1634. Essex House took its name from Robert Devereux, Earl of Essex; it had originally been the town house or inn of the Bishop of Exeter, on land leased from the Knights Templar. There were successively two palaces called Cecil House, one on the north side of the Strand (where the Strand Palace Hotel now stands), the other on the south (site of Shell-Mex House); the former was built for Queen Elizabeth's minister Lord Burghley, the latter by his son, Robert Cecil, Earl of Salisbury, around the turn of the seventeenth century: it was also known as Salisbury House. The Earl of Bedford's house stood on the North side; its garden became what is now Covent Garden.

Somerset House, Northumberland House and Hungerford House will come later in the book. Here it is enough to describe, as a representative sample, two of the most striking of the palaces: the Savoy and York (Villiers) House.

The Savoy was one of the great palaces of Europe. Its name derives from Peter of Savoy, the uncle of Eleanor of Aquitaine, wife of Henry III — 'a civilised, strong and attractive character,' according to the writer Compton Mackenzie; at Eleanor's behest, the King, in 1246, gave Peter the land between the Strand and the Thames. Eleanor subsequently bought the manor back and gave it to her second son, Edmund, Earl of Lancaster. It then descended to his grandson Henry, Earl of Lancaster and Derby, who had enriched himself from the booty of Bergerac in the Dordogne, which he captured for Edward

III. Created Duke of Lancaster, he enlarged his landholding and began to build. There were two courts, private apartments facing inwards, rather than overlooking the Thames, a cloister and the usual extensive services — bakehouse, brewery, laundry, smithy, stables, fishpond, various gardens; the aptly named Nicholas Gardiner tended the vegetable garden. All his riches, however, were not sufficient to prevent the Duke from succumbing to plague at Leicester in 1361.

The Duke's daughter, Blanche, inherited all his estates, including the Savoy, which therefore became home to her husband, John of Gaunt, son of Edward III. He was also created Duke of Lancaster; the ground on which the Savoy palace was built has remained in the possession of the Duchy of Lancaster ever since. During Edward III's last illness and after his death in 1377, John of Gaunt became the effective ruler of England, during the minority of his elder brother, the Black Prince's son, Richard II. It was not a happy time for the country, as Gaunt led a fruitless but costly siege of the French port of Saint-Malo. To recoup the expense of the French wars, Parliament was cajoled into imposing the first of a number of poll taxes, levying a charge of one groat (4d) on all lay people over the age of sixteen — a measure which bore particularly heavily on those least able to pay.

The Savoy was now 'a lodging unrivalled in splendour and nobility within the kingdom.' We know that, because it is how the palace was described when it was burnt to the ground during the Peasants' Revolt of 1381. Supporters of the Duke were badly beaten or killed. Five wagonloads of furnishings, plate and jewels were heaped onto a costly bonfire: so loathed was he that the mob preferred to destroy, rather than loot, his possessions. This was thirsty work, and it was said that thirty-two rebels repaired to the cellars where they became trapped; despite cries for help, they died in the ensuing fire.

The palace could not be rebuilt in Gaunt's lifetime. Lead was taken away to be used on Hertford Castle. For over a century, the palace stood in ruins. Its name, however, survives in the Savoy Hotel and Theatre which occupy a small part of the site (see Chapter Seven).

York House had been built for the Bishop of Norwich, before being granted to the

> 'All his riches, were not sufficient to prevent the Duke from succumbing to plague at Leicester in 1361.'

FIG 6
York Water Gate and the Adelphi from the River, *John O'Connor, 1872. Somerset House and the Adelphi wharves are visible in the background.*

*York House was built for the Bishop of Norwich, before being granted to the Archbishop of York. The Watergate, built by Nicholas Stone for the 1st Duke of Buckingham in the 1620s, is the only trace of the palaces that once lined the Thames to hint at their splendour. It is emblazoned with Buckingham's coat-of-arms, as well as anchors to indicate that he was Lord High Admiral of England.*

*Now landlocked in Embankment Gardens, a hundred and fifty yards inland from the Thames, the Watergate marks the point of the old river bank, before the building of the Victoria Embankment in the 1860s.*

Archbishop of York. In 1622, James I granted it — after compensating the then Archbishop of York — to his favourite, George Villiers, 1$^{st}$ Duke of Buckingham. Buckingham, an inveterate buyer of land and builder of houses, modernised his new possession, constructing a suitably princely entrance for his watermen and guests in the York Watergate, emblazoned with his coat-of-arms, as well as anchors to indicate that he was Lord High Admiral of England. Inside York House, Buckingham displayed the superb collection of pictures, sculptures and curiosities which he had acquired. 'When I am contemplating the treasures of rarities which your excellency has in so short a time amassed,' gasped the Duke's advisor, the architect Sir Balthasar Gerbier in 1625, 'I cannot but feel astonishment in the midst of my joy; for out of all the amateurs and princes and kings there is not one who has collected in forty years as many pictures as your excellency has collected in five!'

Buckingham's taste was for the sumptuous. In the hall of York House hung a copy of Titian's equestrian portrait of Charles V which he had seen in Spain, visited during a misguided attempt to secure the Infanta in marriage for his friend, the future Charles I, who went with him. He commissioned a portrait of himself on horseback from Rubens. No doubt he consulted John Tradescant the Elder, whom he employed as his gardener, about some of his purchases: Tradescant's museum in Vauxhall, one of the earliest in the country, would become the basis of the Ashmolean Museum in Oxford.

After disastrous attempts to attack Cadiz in Spain and the Ile de Ré in France, Buckingham was assassinated by one of his former troops. His son, also George, was only seven months old at the time. Charles I took him into his family and he grew up with the royal princes, the future Charles II and James II. After the Civil War, Cromwell gave York House to the parliamentary general Thomas Fairfax, whose daughter had married the 2$^{nd}$ Duke of Buckingham. At the Restoration, it passed to the 2$^{nd}$ Duke himself, a magnifico like his father, but — again like his father — he was plagued by debt and had to sell: 'In squandering wealth was his peculiar art,' wrote Dryden. In 1672 the 2$^{nd}$ Duke of Buckingham sold York House to developers with the proviso that every part of his name should be remembered in the ensuing streets. We have, therefore, George Street, Villiers Street, Duke Street and Buckingham Street, as well as Of Alley — its name changed by an unimaginative Westminster City Council to York Place in the twentieth century (although the street sign bears the words, in small capitals, 'FORMERLY OF ALLEY', to mystify the

# Chapter Two
## *The Road*

Then there was the road, because some journeys were, of necessity, made by land. A memory of one of them stands outside Charing Cross Station, at the western end of the Strand. It is a reproduction of a medieval cross. The original was a very sophisticated piece of Gothic workmanship, commissioned by the King himself, Edward I, after the death of his beloved Queen Eleanor in 1290.

Edward and Eleanor were unusual in the annals of royal matrimony: they genuinely loved each other. Eleanor was frequently with the King on his campaigns. At Acre, she is supposed to have sucked the poison from a wound he suffered. She had been on the way to join him as he battled the Scots when she was taken ill at Harby in Nottinghamshire. Edward hurried South, arriving in time to witness her death. He was so overcome that he personally led the funeral cortege back to London as chief mourner. It says something about the state of the roads in Edward's kingdom that the journey took nearly a fortnight. The route was dictated by the royal houses and monasteries where the King and his retinue could spend the night. Later, at each of these stopping places Edward erected an elaborate cross. The last of them was placed on land owned by an Augustinian nunnery, where the equestrian statue Charles I now stands at the base of Trafalgar Square. The idea grew up that Charing Cross took its name from chère reigne — dear queen: a pretty story, though unfortunately false.

If Edward I, or any of the medieval monarchs, had gone east towards Ludgate, he would have found the route muddy and difficult to negotiate, being crossed by innumerable rivulets and streams. Officially, the Strand is part of the A4, the Great West Road that runs all the way to Bristol. It must always have been an important thoroughfare, linking the court at Westminster with the merchants of the City of

London. But before the sixteenth century the Strand was little more than a track. In fact the various references in official documents describe it as practically impassable in bad weather. In 1532, an Act of Parliament was passed to have it paved. Whatever work was carried out did not make a lasting impression. As late as 1765, the visiting Frenchman Pierre-Jean Grosley could still write of

> 'I saw, during the whole of my stay in London, the middle of the street constantly adorned with a liquid, noxious mud.'

it as a linear mire. 'For the greater part of the Strand, towards St Clement's church,' he reports in *Londres*, 'I saw, during the whole of my stay in London, the middle of the street constantly adorned with a liquid, noxious mud, to the height of three or four inches: mud whose spray covered pedestrians from head to foot, filling carriages whose glass was not raised, and daubing the ground floors of houses exposed to it.' Improvement, however, was on its way.

The first harbinger of better times had come in the Jacobean period. In 1609, a spectacular new shopping experience was created on land that had previously been occupied by the dilapidated stables of Durham House, one of the Thames-side palaces (see page 32). This was formally called the New Exchange, backed by Lord Salisbury to the tune of £10,000. The object was to provide somewhere that the goods being imported by the new East India Company could be sold. It was to be a meeting place where people congregate, linger and, while they were at it, buy something. Perhaps for the first time in England, the psychology of the shopper had been studied and understood. The advent of such a luxurious emporium in this western location rattled the shopkeepers of the City, who sent Lord Salisbury a petition objecting to 'a Pawne or Exchange for the sale of things usually uttered in the Royal Exchange, and which, being situated near to Whitehall and in the highway, would...tend to the destruction of trade.' This bleat was ignored, and when James I opened the New Exchange on April 11, 1609, he called it 'Britain's Burse.' The name stuck.

Britain's Burse was a success. Like other meeting places, it acquired a reputation for immoral assignations, and Samuel Pepys used it for that purpose; but he was also there buying anything from knives and cloth to baubles, dressing boxes and books. City commerce was right to worry: the trade in luxury goods had begun its inexorable march west.

Two monuments of architecture arose

FIG 7 (LEFT) AND 8 (RIGHT)
*St Clement Danes blazes after being bombed during the Second World War. Right hand image shows the church today. The spire of Wren's church was designed by James Gibbs.*

FIG 9 (BELOW)
*Built in 1714-23, Gibbs's St Mary le Strand replaced a church that had been demolished by Protector Somerset to improve his palace of Somerset House in the mid 16th century*

when the churches of St Clement Danes and St Mary le Strand were rebuilt. The architect of St Clement Danes was Sir Christopher Wren, who had recently rebuilt, with astounding invention, fifty-one of the City churches destroyed in the Great Fire of London. St Clement Danes had escaped the Fire; but the old church was presumably decayed, and certainly not as convenient as the churches that had become the ornament of the rebuilt City. Its position on the route from Westminster to St Paul's, often taken by processions, exposed it to comment. The old church was taken down in 1680 and the new one erected on a slightly different site. In one respect it is unique: St Clement Danes is the only one of Wren's churches to have an apse. In other ways, its shape — a nave with barrel vault and aisles — corresponds to other Wren churches, such as St Bride's, Fleet Street and St James's, Piccadilly. Like St Bride's and St James's, St Clement Danes has a gallery that is part of the architecture, not an afterthought added to provide more space. Light pours in through tall, round headed windows that rise into cross vaults.

'While the spire of St Clement Danes was ascending elegantly heavenwards, a complete new church was rising a little way to the west.'

Victorian parishioners placed an inscription to remember a distinguished worshipper from the eighteenth century:

*In this pew and beside this pillar, for many years attended divine service the celebrated Dr. Samuel Johnson, the philosopher, the poet, the great lexicographer, the profound moralist, and chief writer of his time. Born 1709, died 1784. In the remembrance and honour of noble faculties, nobly employed, some inhabitants of the parish of St. Clement Danes have placed this slight memorial, AD 1851.*

Johnson compiled his Dictionary nearby, at 17 Gough Square. When the church was gutted by fire during the Blitz, his pew was destroyed. However, the great man of letters, bewigged and reading from a book, still walks the Strand in the shape of a bronze statue outside. The church was rebuilt in 1958 by the Royal Air Force, who have adopted it as their spiritual home.

Wren did not design the spire of St Clement's; that was added by James Gibbs in 1719. Its lively silhouette and restless geometry reflect the time that Gibbs had spent in Baroque

FIG 10
*Samuel Johnson in a statue by Percy Hetherington Fitzgerald, unveiled in 1910. Johnson, literary giant and famous conversationalist, lived off the Strand in Gough Square.*

Rome. Ten bells had been cast in 1693. They dispute the honour of being the Bells of St Clement's mentioned in the nursery rhyme Oranges and Lemons with the Church of St Clement Eastcheap. Before services, the bells are run as peals, but there is also — unusually for London — a carillon which plays well-known tunes; the carillon is an introduction of the 1920s.

While the spire of St Clement Danes was ascending elegantly heavenwards, a complete new church was rising a little way to the west: St Mary le Strand, also designed by Gibbs. The church was the reassertion of the will of the parish, after a scandal perpetrated a hundred and seventy-five years before. One of the magnates to have built a Thames-side palace was the Lord Protector during Edward VI's childhood, Edward Seymour, Duke of Somerset, the brother of Henry VIII's last wife, Jane Seymour. His architectural appetite was prodigious. To enlarge the site of the palace, he ordered the church of St Mary, which stood on the Strand, to be taken down; its stones were then used in the new building, along with others from a cloister at St Paul's Cathedral known as Pardon Churchyard, and the Priory of St John at Clerkenwell. Although Somerset may have vowed to rebuild St Mary's, he never did, and the intention died with his beheading in 1552.

Dispossessed, St Mary's parishioners regrouped at the Chapel of St John the Baptist, part of the hospital that Henry VII built over the ruins of John of Gaunt's Savoy palace; its name changed to St Mary le Savoy. (The chapel survives — see Chapter Seven). There, they would have heard the witty churchman and writer, Thomas Fuller, a Royalist who was compelled to leave in 1643 (he joined the King in Oxford), to be reinstated at the Restoration seventeen years later.

When an Act of Parliament was passed to build fifty new churches in the expanding suburbs of London in 1711, the congregation of St Mary's was quick to apply for funds. Although Roman Catholic, Gibbs, as a Tory, was regarded sympathetically by the then government, as well as the congregation. The new site, at the point where the Strand bellied out to pass on either side of it, had, since the Middle Ages, been occupied by an elaborate cross. There was also the most famous maypole in London. This was torn down by the Puritans,

FIG 11
*The Savoy Chapel. On land owned by the Duchy of Lancaster, the Chapel is the last surviving building of a hospital founded by Henry VII for homeless people, the construction of which was completed in 1512 a few years after his death. The hospital was built on the ruins of the palace owned by John of Gaunt, Duke of Lancaster.*

*The Savoy Chapel belongs to Her Majesty The Queen in her right as Duke of Lancaster. It is a 'free' chapel or 'peculiar' because it does not fall within any bishop's jurisdiction, while remaining firmly within the Church of England.*

# Durham House

Durham House, or Durham Inn, was one of several palaces beside the river Thames, built by important churchmen — in this case, the Bishop of Durham — for use during their time at the court in London. By the mid-thirteenth century Durham House had become a 'noble pile.' Over the next century it grew even more sumptuous. It was at Durham House that Catherine of Aragon took up residence after the death of her first husband, Prince Arthur, surrounded by rich tapestries and hangings, and attended by fifty Spanish followers. So much opulence was irresistible to Cardinal Wolsey, who had himself appointed Prince-Bishop of Durham, in addition to his many other preferments. Both Anne Boleyn's father, Sir Thomas Boleyn, and the future queen herself stayed at Durham House before Wolsey's fall. After the Cardinal's death, Henry VIII himself now made use of it for entertainments and feasting. Later, when the house was in the possession of John Dudley, Earl of Warwick and Duke of Northumberland, it was from the steps of Durham House that Lady Jane Grey left for the royal palace of the Tower of London, for a reign that lasted only nine days.

John Aubrey, writing in the late seventeenth century, remembered Durham House as 'a noble

Drawn by Nathaniel Smith 1790 & etched by J T Smith.

*Durham House, Strand.*

FIG 12
*Durham House, engraving
by John Thomas Smith, 1806*

palace.' Sir Walter Raleigh, during a time of favour with Elizabeth I, had occupied it, using, for his study, 'a little turret that looked into and over the Thames, and had the prospect which is, perhaps, as pleasant as any in the world.'

but a new one was erected during the return to merrymaking at the Restoration. The maypole survived until 1717 when wood from it was presented to Sir Isaac Newton as the base to a telescope.

Because of its prominent position, St Mary le Strand was made sumptuous. Gibbs, born in Aberdeen in 1682, had originally been destined for the Roman Catholic priesthood — hence his journey to Rome. Once there he turned to architecture, studying with the prolific Baroque architect Carlo Fontana. Having returned to Britain in 1709, Gibbs became, through the manoeuvring of a fellow Scot, the Earl of Mar, one of the two surveyors to the Commission for Building Fifty New Churches. He began St Mary le Strand in 1714. The original design had no spire. Instead a tall column to Queen Anne was to stand in front of the church. This was abandoned when Queen Anne died in 1714. Her death also signalled a change in Gibbs's fortunes, and St Mary le Strand would be the only church that he built for the Commission. The Jacobite uprising of 1715 created political difficulty for a Scot and Roman Catholic such as Gibbs. For all that, St Mary le Strand, with its double tier of Orders and semi-circular porch, reminiscent of Santa Maria della Pace in Rome, made Gibbs' reputation. Among other churches, country houses and university buildings that he went on to design is St Martin-in-the-Fields, 1722-26, its name denoting that the area around what would become Trafalgar Square was still a rural location.

The loss of the maypole was mourned, facetiously, by the clergyman James Bramston, in his Art of Politicks, 1729 (praised by no less an authority than Alexander Pope); near the church could be found waiting hackney coaches which took

> ...their stand,
> Where the tall maypole o'erlooked the Strand;
> And now — so Anne and Piety ordain —
> A church collects the saints of Drury Lane...
> What's not destroyed by Time's devouring hand?
> Where's Troy — and where's the Maypole in the Strand?

The saints of Drury Lane were the prostitutes for which the area around Covent Garden was notorious.

But the Strand was not only a haunt of low life. The splendid new churches of St Clement Danes and St Mary le Strand reflect

## 'What's not destroyed by Time's devouring hand? Where's Troy — and where's the Maypole in the Strand?'

the emergence of a prosperous residential district. The course had been set by the 4th Earl of Bedford who commissioned Inigo Jones to develop the garden of his house on the Strand in the 1630s as Covent Garden. Jones devised an Italianate square or piazza, inspired by the Place des Voges in Paris. This included an arcade for strolling and the church of St Paul, whose deep, shady Tuscan portico might have been designed for a sunnier climate than that of London; neither proved particularly influential. But the innovation which the English took to heart was the terrace, joining vertically separate houses together to form a continuous row. In the second half of the seventeenth century, a supply of building plots was released by the decay of the palaces off the Strand. Badly treated under the Commonwealth, they were becoming too remote from the seats of power to be rebuilt. The Tower of London had long ceased to be used as a royal palace, and William and Mary moved west, to Kensington Palace, where the drier air suited William's asthma. The coup de grace, as far as the aristocracy was concerned, came with the fire that destroyed all of Whitehall Palace except for the Banqueting House in 1698. So the magnificent halls that had housed the mightiest prelates, princes and courtiers of the land were redeveloped as dwellings for the middle classes.

'Barbon was an adventurer with nerves of steel and a complete disregard for the opinions of his contemporaries. He would be called rogue, knave, damned Barbon, or anything, without being moved...'

The pioneer, in the 1670s, was Nicholas Barbon. An indication of the religious temper of his background can be judged from his middle name, Unless-Jesus-Christ-Had-Died-For-Thee-Thou-Hadst-Been-Damned — a development of his father's Christian name of Praisegod. Praisegod Barbon was a leather merchant and politician, after whom the brief 'Barebone' Parliament of 1653 was named. Unlike his father, Nicholas Barbon lived richly, having developed a number of mechanisms to help London recover from the Great Fire of London, including fire insurance, mortgages and house building. Like house builders and speculators in other ages, he was an adventurer with nerves of steel and a complete disregard for the opinions

FIG 13

*The Adam Brothers' Adelphi, unknown artist. The lowest level of the Adelphi consisted of warehouses, which could be reached by boat. They were given Diocletian windows of the kind seen in the enormous baths of Ancient Rome and the fourth-century palace of the Emperor Diocletian in what is now Croatia (Robert Adam had studied it on his travels). The embankment distanced the fashionable development from some of the objectionable aspects of the river; it also protected the houses against flooding.*

of his contemporaries — one of whom wrote that 'he would be called rogue, knave, damned Barbon, or anything, without being moved.' He did, however, get things done, 'being surpassed only by Nash in his influence on the appearance of London,' according to Peter Ackroyd. One of his projects was to build on George Street, Villiers Street, Duke Street, Buckingham Street and Of Alley on the site of what had been York House; they were collectively known as York Buildings. For a winter, the diarist John Evelyn took a house there; as did Samuel Pepys, living for many years in some state in Buckingham Street. 'I know that next to the King's business you have full employment in furnishing your new house,' his friend James Houblon wrote to him. As the *Survey of London* (volume XVIII) found in 1937, a surprising amount of the original seventeenth century work survives in Buckingham Street, although most of the houses were then in commercial rather than domestic use.

FIG 14
*Robert Adam, by George Willison, circa 1770.*

*Adam, an ambitious as well as fashionable architect who worked for patrons whom he had often met on the Grand Tour, joined his brothers James and John in developing the Adelphi (Greek for 'brothers') in 1768-74. It was an ingenious and bold scheme, which created several new streets, composed to read as palaces, above an embankment of the Thames. The scheme very nearly bankrupted the family.*

A house of a few decades later can be seen in Craven Street, whose shape derives from its predecessor, Spur Alley. It was erected around 1730. In 1757, Benjamin Franklin, sent to London as a diplomat for the Pennsylvania Assembly, took lodgings at 36 Craven Street, now a museum. Sash windows are taller, glazing bars thinner; the ground floor is stucco-fronted and coursed to resemble stone.

Fashion descended on a more ambitious scale in 1768-74, with the buildings of the Adelphi. Adelphi, in Greek, means 'brothers', and the entrepreneurs in this case were Robert Adam and his brothers, James and John. Their site was that of Durham House, a palace that had begun its existence as the 'inn' of the Prince-Bishop of Durham, whose see was also a county palatine (in which the Prince-Bishop had quasi-regal powers to hold the border against the Scots). Its splendour was irresistible to Cardinal Wolsey, Henry VIII and Edward VI's mentor, the 'wicked' Duke of Northumberland, promoter of Lady Jane Grey.

By the eighteenth century, those glories had long faded, and the Adams acquired a lease of the site from the then owner, the Duke of St Albans, for ninety-nine years. Robert Adam, already established with a fashionable practice building country houses for the young noblemen whom he had met on the Grand Tour, was the architect. It was an ingenious scheme — and very bold. Although largely composed of individual dwelling houses, the design read as one structure, organised on a series of terraces supported on vaults. On the ground floor, fronting the river, were warehouses, given Diocletian windows of the kind seen in the enormous baths of Ancient Rome and the 4th century palace of the Emperor Diocletian in what is now Croatia (Robert Adam had studied it on his travels). Extra space was won from the river by embanking it. This made the foreshore more palatable to the Georgian nose, less robust than the medieval one, by distancing the noisome burden of the river that was exposed at low tide; it also protected the houses against flooding. Several new streets were created — Adelphi Terrace, Adam Street, Robert Street and John Street.

When Robert Adam had entered practice a decade before, he brought to architecture a lighter, almost nervous style, whose elements were derived as much from painted decoration, as discovered in Pompeii and Herculaneum, as from the Classical monuments of antiquity. The brick façades of the houses above them were enlivened with stucco ornaments — pilaster strips, entablatures and string courses. The ironwork of balconies, railing, lamp standards and fanlights was delicate and feminine.

In John Street, a more substantial design fronted the Royal Society of Arts (the Society for the Encouragement of Arts, Manufacturers and Commerce, as it was called when established in 1754). The Society held the first organised art exhibition in the country in 1760. Adam dignified the façade with a temple front of attached Ionic columns, framing a Palladian window topped with a fan motif. For the Great Room, the artist James Barry painted a cycle of allegorical murals to embody the Society's preoccupations, the subjects of which were *Orpheus, A Grecian Harvest-Home, Crowning the Victors at Olympia, Commerce or the Triumph of the Thames, The Distribution of Premiums in the Society of Arts* and *Elysium, or the State of Final*

'Robert Adam, already established with a fashionable practice building country houses for the young noblemen whom he had met on the Grand Tour, was the architect. It was an ingenious scheme — and very bold.'

FIG 15

*The Royal Society of Arts begin life as the Society for the Encouragement of Arts, Manufacturers and Commerce in 1754. It held the first organised art exhibition in the country in 1760. For the Great Room, the artist James Barry painted a cycle of allegorical murals to embody the Society's preoccupations, the subjects of which were* Orpheus, A Grecian Harvest-Home, Crowning the Victors at Olympia, Commerce, or the Triumph of the Thames, The Distribution of Premiums in the Society of Arts *and* Elysium, or the State of Final Retribution.

*Retribution* — a programme that was almost as ambitious artistically as the Adelphi itself, although perhaps less successful.

Commercially, the Adelphi was a disaster and nearly bankrupted the Adams. Their business methods had been cavalier. They did not so much as sign their lease until a year after work had started. Permission to embank the Thames was more difficult to obtain than they had imagined. The Ordnance Office, whom they had confidentially expected to lease all the vaults as warehouses, failed to do so. By 1773 they had exhausted their capital. It was only by holding a lottery, with some of the houses as prizes, that they were able to rescue their fortunes. Their streets did not become quite the prestige addresses that they had hoped. Smart London had turned its back on the river, and it remained turned (at least downstream) until the riverside developments, often occupied by foreigners, of the late twentieth century.

Although the Adams' terrace survives — and its vaults provide motorists with a rare moment of sublimity on a London street, akin to driving through one of Piranesi's Carceri engravings — the Adelphi was mistreated in the nineteenth century and largely destroyed in the twentieth. Only one of the houses has come down to us in anything like its original condition — 11 Adelphi Terrace, the shop of coin dealers A H Baldwin and Sons. For all that, the Adelphi was a brave venture. It demonstrated the benefit of embanking the Thames, a century before the Victorians did so more thoroughly. It also transformed the western end of the Strand. The result may not have been quite as exclusive as the Adams had hoped, but, by that very fact, it gave pleasure to a greater number of people. The Strand could be elegant, but it remained middle class. This character was confirmed by the extraordinary building that soon appeared next to St Mary le Strand.

# Chapter Three

## *Somerset House*

One of the most ostentatious of the Tudor and Stuart Thames palaces had been Somerset House. It had been built by Edward Seymour, 1st Duke of Somerset, who, as Lord Protector during the minority of Edward VI, had regal powers over the kingdom. This, as well as personal ambition, required him to have a palace suitable to his status, in which he could make decisions, issue commands, send out instructions, meet the many individuals wanting to gain his attention and house his retinue. John Norden showed the house as he left it in his map of Westminster, made at the end of the century. We see a great court, an inner court and what appears to be a pile of building rubble, suggesting that, dynamo that he was, Somerset did not have time to complete his project. The tale of the Lord Protector's demise is succinctly told by the young King Edward in the *Chronicle* that he kept: 'the Duke of Somerset had his head cut off upon Tower Hill between eight and nine o'clock in the morning.'

From the Stuart period, Somerset House was particularly associated with England's Queens. As Simon Thurley has written, James I's queen, Anne of Denmark, transformed it into 'one of the great buildings of seventeenth-century England: great architecturally, but also important as a cultural centre and as one of the pivots upon which royal London turned.' There are drawings by John Thorpe associated with her work, although it is uncertain how much of what they show was built. Quite apart from the architectural and social magnificence of the palace, the tenements on the Strand that went with it provided a useful income for the queen.

> 'From the Stuart period, Somerset House was particularly associated with England's Queens.'

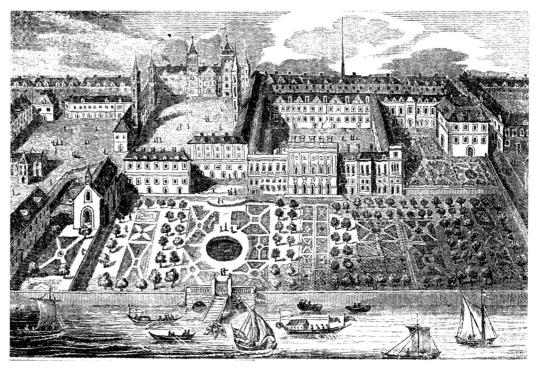

FIG 16
*Old Somerset House,
engraving, by Wenceslaus
Hollar (1607-1677). Note
the Strand maypole in the
background.*

In the next reign, Charles I gave Somerset House to Queen Henrietta-Maria who, being French, had a developed sense of style in all visual matters. She did nothing for her husband's popularity by building a Roman Catholic chapel, served by a bishop, a confessor, musicians and twelve Capuchin friars (although it was better to have one at Somerset House than to use the chapel at St James's Chapel for Popery). During the Commonwealth, when some of the royal properties were sold and the royal collections dispersed, Oliver Cromwell found that he needed Somerset House to fulfil certain purposes of state, such as the reception of ambassadors. It was here that his own body lay in state. When Henrietta Maria made her return after the Restoration, she swept in, 'a very plain little old woman,' according to Pepys, dressed always in black. The colour, however, was not unbecoming, and her twenty-four menservants, in their cassocks of black velvet, embroidered with golden suns, must

FIG 17
Fountains in the courtyard of Somerset
House in May 2014: an oasis of art and
architecture in the centre of London.
Not so long ago it was a car park for the
Inland Revenue

FIG 18
*One of the many purposes to which Somerset House can now be put is the filming of period drama: here it provides the background to a Victorian street scene.*

have looked striking. The centre block on the river side was rebuilt by John Webb, in the style of his hero Inigo Jones's Queen's House at Greenwich: 'mighty magnificent and costly,' was Pepys's judgment. A century later, however, Queen Charlotte, George III's wife, did not use Somerset House, preferring Buckingham House (now Palace). Then in 1774 its fate was sealed: large parts of it collapsed. The King had the site cleared.

Ever since the burning of Whitehall Palace in 1698, civil servants had been short of office space. Two great departments of state had been housed in the course of the eighteenth century, with a new Treasury Building and Horse Guards Parade for the military. The Royal Navy, however, was poorly served — and Britain was a maritime power. It was principally for the Admiralty's benefit that a new complex of offices was conceived. A rag tag of other government functions, as well as a number of learned societies, were also given shelter within a scheme that, in the Classical age, could accommodate many different uses behind coolly unified façades.

Fortunately for the course of British architecture, William Robinson died of gout in 1775. Robinson was a pedestrian architect, whose work on various official projects is unremembered. He had succeeded in wangling the job to design the new Somerset House. His death made way for a man of genius, William Chambers, then somewhat underemployed (who, being Robinson's senior in the Office of Works, should have got the commission in the first place.)

Before we admire Chambers's new building, let us linger for a moment in the old one, as it was found when a party inspected it shortly before demolition.

*In one part were the vestiges of a throne and canopy of state; in another curtains for the audience chamber, which had once been crimson velvet, fringed with gold . . . With respect to the gold and silver which were worked in the borders of the tapestries with which the royal apartments were, even within my remembrance, hung, it had been carefully picked out while those rooms had been used as barracks... The audience chamber had been hung with silk, which was in tatters, as were the curtains, gilt leather covers, and painted screens. . . The general state of this building, its mouldering walls and decaying furniture, broken casements, falling roof, and the long range of its uninhabited and uninhabitable apartments, presented to the mind in strong, though gloomy, colours a correct picture of those dilapidated castles, the haunts of spectres and residence of magicians and murderers, which have since the period to which I allude made such a figure in romance.*

Those ghosts were banished, as Chambers and his employers debated the opulence or parsimony with which his new building would be constructed. Magnificence versus economy — it is an eternal debate in government projects. Chambers was determined to build a palace for civil servants, and won the backing of his paymasters. Built of one piece, it would outshine its predecessors on the site.

None of the old palaces had their principal front towards the Strand, and Somerset House was no exception. The space for a Strand entrance was limited; Chambers made the most of it with a neoclassical façade in the French style, inspired by the recently built Hôtel des Monnaies in Paris. Three arches give into a vestibule with paired columns and vaults, creating an impression of airy lightness despite the limited extend. The vestibule opens into a large courtyard. On the river front, Chambers followed the Adams' example by embanking the Thames. Rising out of the water, the bottom level was composed of bold rustication, with river entrances flanked by pairs of columns, banded with vermiculation; the vermiculation — a way of treating stone to make it look as though it is covered with worm casts — must have looked as though it had something in common with the river bed. Above was a terrace, the whole of which was faced with a façade of prodigious length, broken by the project of centrepiece and pavilions. Long and low, it is marked in the centre by a pediment and dome. The effect was palatial and cool: in mass Palladian, in detail French.

Among the occupants were the Royal Society, the Society of Antiquaries and the Royal Academy; they were given pride of place in the Strand block. Vaults beneath them were intended for the repository of public records. The Navy Office was accommodated in the western half of the range overlooking the river; near them, in the west range, were the Sick and Hurt, Navy Pay and Victualling Offices, while the eastern half of the river front was occupied by the Stamp Office. Rooms were also found for the Duchy of Cornwall and a medley of other bureaucratic institutions, such the Office of Hawkers and Pedlars, the Hackney Coach Office. In addition, some of the most senior servants of the State — the Commissioners of the Navy and Victualling Offices — required houses. A terrace of nine official dwellings was constructed in a terrace west of the courtyard.

Most of the activities performed in the new Somerset House were administrative, rather than ceremonial, and all the money to pay for the building came from the Treasury. Nevertheless, Chambers succeeded in investing the complex with refinement, sometimes drama. The Seamen's Hall, where Nelson and his commanders waited, is staunchly Doric, the most masculine of the Classical orders; but the staircase up which they walked to the office of the Navy Board, to discover which ships they had been given, flies lightly up through an oval space, lit from above. A double flight of stairs is followed by a straight 'flying flight' (over a void); then the last of the three flights curls around the wall. Elsewhere, light wells and changes of level are exploited to almost theatrical effect; but such episodes are few.

The qualities of Somerset House are balance and restraint. This can be seen in details such as the ironwork, whose curling motifs are as poised as a Jane Austen heroine in a quadrille; the shapes are abstracted from the anthemions and volutes of Classical architecture.

Somerset House continued to be used by the civil service — in particular, HM Revenue and Customs — into the early part of the twenty-

FIG 19
*The former entrance to the
Inland Revenue Offices at
Somerset House, a palace built
for civil servants.*

first century. With peculiar insensitivity to the architecture, the courtyard became used as a car park. This provided a perk which the bureaucrats were reluctant to forego. But it was eventually wrested from their grasp and Chambers's great building made over to the Somerset House Trust. The courtyard has since been restored and opened up to new life, whether that may be ice-skating at Christmastime, delighting children with tricksy fountains in hot weather or the filming of period dramas.

## King's College London

Chambers had not been able to complete his vision for Somerset House. At his death in 1796, one of the side pieces which he had envisaged remained unbuilt. The government, however, owned the land. A use occurred for one wing in

1829, when the Prime Minister and the Duke of Wellington championed a project.

In 1828, University College — the first University of London — was opened by a group of Non-Conformists and avowed atheists. Students at Oxford and Cambridge could only take a degree if they subscribed to the Thirty-Nine Articles which defined the doctrine of the Church of England. University College offered a secular alternative, open to anyone, regardless of religion, who could afford the fees. Conservatives saw this, correctly, as a challenge to their own cherished beliefs. Their riposte was to establish their own college in London. King's College, as the name declared, would be true to the King and the Church of which he was head. University College had raised a building of Greek Revival purity on a large site in Bloomsbury. King's College, with a front overlooking the Thames and a position next to the learned societies in Somerset House, was equally prominent.

Whereas University College had chosen William Wilkins, architect of Downing College, Cambridge, as well as the National Gallery, as their architect, the promoters of King's College turned to Robert Smirke. Smirke had a large practice building country houses, clubs and institutions, such as the British Museum. On the river front, he confined himself to completing Chambers's design, building a separate pavilion to the east of the main block, linked by a columnar screen over an arched river entrance. This was faced with Portland stone, which London's notorious atmosphere soon darkened to tone with the original. Most of the accommodation for King's College was built of utilitarian brick. More remarkable for its use of cast-iron supports than its decoration, it stood at right angles to the river, facing a narrow courtyard; in the basement was King's College School (it decamped to healthy Wimbledon Common in 1897). Smirke's gateway was demolished in 1972 to make way for a new Strand block in the Brutalist style by E D Jefferiss Mathews.

Today, King's College occupies no fewer than five campuses in and around London, with the Strand Campus spread across four sites, including James Pennethorne's old Public Records Office on Chancery Lane, now Maughan Library. The arrival of the London School of Economics will be described in Chapter Eight; here it is enough to note that together the two institutions have given Northbank the character of an academic district, adding to the vitality of the urban scene.

FIG 20 (LEFT) AND 21 (BELOW)
*Two of the four campuses that King's College, London, occupies in and around the Strand: above, the old Public Record Office on Chancery Lane by James Pennethorne, now the Maughan Library; below, the reinforced concrete and plate glass of E D Jefferiss Matthews's Brutalist frontage to the Strand, which replaced a gateway by Robert Smirke.*

*With the London School of Economics also occupying several sites around Northbank, the area has become something of an academic* quartier.

# Chapter Four
## *Trafalgar Square*

At the bottom of Trafalgar Square is an equestrian statue of Charles I. It was commissioned from the French sculptor Hubert Le Sueur by the Lord Treasurer, the future Lord Portland, in 1630. Although designed in the spirit of a great public sculpture, in a tradition going back to the statue of Marcus Aurelius on the Capitol in Rome, Portland intended it for a private setting: the garden of his house at Mortlake, to the west of the capital. During the Civil War, Parliament ordered it to be sold and broken up, but after the Restoration it was produced, intact, by John Rivett, the King's Brazier. Out of loyalty, Rivett had buried it, while keeping up a hammering noise in his workshop to pretend that it was being destroyed. This resulted, according to one

> 'Out of loyalty, Rivett had buried the statue, while keeping up a hammering noise in his workshop to pretend that it was being destroyed.'

sceptical writer, in 'a brisk trade in knives and forks, with bronze handles, which he pretended were made out of the obnoxious statue. He clearly must have made a good thing out of the knives and forks which he manufactured in bronze for sale, since the Royalists no doubt eagerly bought them as relics of their unfortunate and lamented sovereign, whilst the Puritans and Roundheads would be equally glad to secure them as trophies of the downfall of a despot.' Returned to Portland's family, the statue was sold by the widow of the 2nd Earl to Charles II in 1675. Looking proudly down Whitehall to the scene of his execution, it became the point from which distances to and from London were measured. Trafalgar Square is the very centre of the capital.

FIG 22

Trafalgar Square, *by James Pollard (1792-1867), unknown date. It was John Nash who proposed the creation of a public square on the site of what had been the stables for Whitehall Palace in the 1820s. This shows the view from Whitehall before the erection of Nelson's column, for which a competition was held in 1838-9. The Square was only named in 1835, thirty years after the Battle of Trafalgar.*

FIG 23

*The National Gallery, with St Martin-in-the-Fields in the background. The National Gallery occupies the site of the stables which William Kent built in 1732. Its architect was the austere Greek Revivalist, William Wilkins. To save money, the portico re-used columns from the Prince Regent's Carlton House, demolished when, as George IV, he moved to Buckingham Palace.*

The square itself is a Victorian creation. Before it came into being, the position of the equestrian statue was highly appropriate: the area was one of palpable horsiness, most of it having been the site of the Royal Mews. The mews had been established by Edward I, who allowed its keeper 9d a day. There was a fire in 1534, which 'brent many great Horses and great store of haye;' after which Henry VIII pillaged the buildings for materials to improve York House. But over £8,000 was spent in rebuilding them in the reigns of Edward VI and Queen Mary. An Elizabethan map, made in connection with a lawsuit, shows the layout, with a long row of stables on the southern side. After the Restoration, Pepys records visiting the Mews, or his coach being diverted through it when a road was blocked, and Sir Christopher Wren drew plans for rebuilding it on a grand scale. They were not carried out. Despite the destruction of Whitehall Palace in the 1690s, the mews continued in use. In 1732, William Kent built a new block of stables on the north side of the square, the site of the National Gallery; a contemporary describes them as being 'in a very singular taste; a mixture of Rustick and Gothique together.' The horses were splendidly housed but not the neighbouring population, and by the beginning of the nineteenth century, some of the surroundings of the Mews — such as Porridge Island — were regarded as squalid. The architect John Nash was the man to take them in hand.

Nash had already conjured Portland Place and Regent Street, running between the Prince of Wales's Regent Street and Carlton House, out of a perplexing number of individually owned properties, on the edge of a slum. In the 1820s, he proposed another civic improvement: that the decayed mews buildings should be swept away to create a large open space, with the National Gallery along the north side. The result was the Charing Cross Improvement Act of 1826. Nothing now survives from Nash's time in Trafalgar Square, although his hand can be seen in a number of buildings at the beginning of the Strand, distinguished by their pepperpot towers and stucco façades.

A competition for the National Gallery was held, and it was won by the austere Greek Revivalist William Wilkins. Politically, the project survived the storms that preceded the passing of the Great Reform Act of 1832, but Wilkins faced other challenges: his building had, like Somerset House, to house some of the public records and the Royal Academy as well as the newly formed collection of pictures (although another home for the records was found before the building was finished). It was expected that the central portico would be composed of columns rescued from Carlton House, the Prince Regent's opulent palace, demolished when he became King and transferred to Buckingham Palace. Furthermore, the clearing of the mews site had revealed Gibbs's church of St Martin-in-the-Fields: surely it would be too painful to obscure it again. Wilkins, by temperament a scholar, was not a man of decision. Although exquisite in detail, his National Gallery has been criticised for not sufficiently dominating the square. That misses the point that the square had not been built at the time that it went up. Instead, the Gallery steps politely back, so as not to block the view of Gibbs's St Martin-in-the-Fields from Pall Mall; following the dictates of the Picturesque Movement, it is best appreciated from Pall Mall — side on, rather than frontally. The massing of Wilkins's structure reads as a succession of projections and recessions — crowned, yes, by a Corinthian portico, but subservient to another portico: that of St Martin's-in-the-Fields. (Although in fairness one must say that preserving the view of the church had been Nash's idea; Wilkins, anxious that his gallery should face down Whitehall, had only been forced to concur when a public outcry was raised by his original proposal).

Until 1835, the square went unnamed; but the idea that it should commemorate the greatest of British sea battles took hold, strengthened by the desire — somewhat late in the day — to commemorate Nelson with a column. By 1840, however, both Nash and Wilkins were dead. It was therefore left to Charles Barry, architect of the Houses of Parliament, to design the square. He proposed a terrace in front of the National Gallery, linked to a lower piazza by stairs, but deplored the idea of a column, on the grounds that it would dwarf both his terrace and Wilkins's building. But Barry was too late. Work on the foundations of the column had already begun. He was forced to accept it.

'Other communities around Britain had been more prompt to show their gratitude in stone.'

The architect of Nelson's Column was William Railton. He had won the public competition held in 1838-39, judged by a committee which included the Duke of Wellington. In the nature of competitions, objections were raised almost as soon as the winner was announced; Railton did make one concession to his critics, reducing the height of the column by twenty feet in case it proved unstable. Even so, work started quickly. Time pressed. It was already more than three decades since Nelson's death. Other communities around Britain had been more prompt to show their gratitude in stone.

Although begun quickly, the work did not continue so. There was a strike of masons, and the granite specified by Railton was hard to obtain. But in 1843 the column was ready to receive its bronze capital, and the statue of Nelson which would go above it. The Illustrated London News reported that the statue weighed eighteen tons and 'will be taken to pieces in order to be put up.' The committee then ran out of money. It was unable to commission the heroic bronze plaques around the base of the column or the four lions that would stand guard. Application was made to the government, in the person of Henry Pelham-Clinton, Lord Lincoln, the future 5th Duke of Newcastle under Lyme. Treasury backing came at a price: Lord Linton had no compunction about interfering with Railton's design, demanding that an

FIG 24
*Nelson's column under construction, April 1844. Photograph by William Henry Fox Talbot (1800-1877).*

elaborate arrangement of steps was omitted, lest it blocked the view of the National Gallery. Railton vigorously objected but eventually buckled; he changed the design of the base. The bronze panels were commissioned, and four lions designed by Sir Edwin Landseer. But when the column was officially opened in 1867, Railton declined to attend the ceremony.

Barry had conceived that Trafalgar Square would be graced by two fountains; by 1845 the number had increased to four. The Builder found them 'exceedingly chaste in design.' The water which fed them came from two artesian wells, one of which was bored in Orange Street, behind the National Gallery, and conveyed by means of a tunnel. However, the Victorian fountains came to be regarded as feeble, and they were replaced in 1939 by the present two fountains by Lutyens, dedicated to the First World War naval commanders, Lord Jellicoe and Lord Beatty. Three statues on granite pedestals or plinths were, in the Victorian period, raised to King George IV (on horseback), George IV, Major-General Sir Henry Havelock (who recaptured Cawnpore during the Indian Rebellion of 1857) and General Sir Charles Napier (a general in India famous for the telegram supposedly sent when he captured Sindh; it consisted of the one Latin word *Peccavi* — I have sinned.) The Fourth Plinth remained empty until it 2007, when it became a showcase for contemporary sculptural commissions, each of which is in occupation for a year or two.

To the *Illustrated London News*, Trafalgar Square was 'magnificent; but it is not such [a square] as woos the pedestrian to repose, or the idler to lounge. In summer, "the sun smites by day, and the cold by night;" and in winter, the biting winds make it equally intolerable.' There were no trees. For the first century and a half of its existence, Trafalgar Square remained an under-used resource, a prime location in the centre of the metropolis, suitable for the holding of rallies but, at other times, windswept and uninviting. It is only in recent years that this space, at the very heart of London, has become somewhere to linger, as shall be told in the final chapter.

FIG 25

*A Merman with Dolphins. There were originally four fountains in Trafalgar Square, fed by artesian wells behind the National Gallery. These were replaced in 1939 by the two that exist today, designed by Sir Edwin Lutyens. They commemorate Admirals Jellicoe and Beatty, and include elaborate sculptures of mermaids, mermen, tritons and dolphins. The sculptures are the work of William McMillan and Sir Charles Wheeler.*

# Chapter Five

## *Structural Strand: Charing Cross Station and Victoria Embankment*

In Tudor times, Charing was a hamlet — just a scattering of modest dwellings and a small church. There was also the Eleanor Cross, which, being so much more of a fine monument than anything else in the immediate neighbourhood, not surprisingly lent its identity to the spot. Charing has been forgotten. Charing Cross has not.

And this is despite the destruction of the cross itself on the orders of Parliament, under the Commonwealth. While standing, the cross had a public role, as a place where public proclamations would be made, and the tradition continued after its destruction. In 1660, the spot was chosen for the execution of three of the regicides who had signed the death warrant of Charles I, including Thomas Harrison; they therefore died within sight of the Banqueting House, outside which the King had been beheaded. As ever, Samuel Pepys was on hand to witness the grisly scene.

*'I went out to Charing Cross to see Major-General Harrison hanged, drawn, and quartered; which was done there, he looking as cheerful as any man could do in that condition. He was presently cut down, and his head and heart shown to the people, at which there was great shouts of joy. ... Thus it was my chance to see the king beheaded at Whitehall, and to see the first blood shed in revenge for the king at Charing Cross.'*

Whatever one might say about the regicides, they were undoubtedly brave.

By contrast, Sir Edward Hugerford, whose family gave their name to Hungerford House, originally the riverside inn of the Bishop of

Norwich, lived to a fine age, dying, after a life of high living and extravagance, in 1711. He was a hundred and fifteen. Hungerford House had burnt spectacularly in 1669, after a servant girl was careless with a bunch of candles, the fire only having been prevented from spreading, according to Pepys, when the adjacent property was blown up. Sir Edward attempted to recoup his fortunes by turning the site into a market — alas, without the desired effect.

> 'The area held no charm for Charles Dickens, who, at the age of twelve, was sent to work in a blacking factory at Hungerford Stairs.'

In the nineteenth century, painters of picturesque views make it look a jolly enough place, the scene enlivened by washing suspended from poles projecting from upper windows of houses. But it held no charm for Charles Dickens, who, at the age of twelve, was sent to work in a blacking factory at Hungerford Stairs. By December 1862, when the *Illustrated London News* published a wood engraving, the scene was one of desolation. The market site was being cleared to make way for Charing Cross Station.

Londoners, Dickens among them, resented the destruction wrought by the railways, which

FIG 26 (ABOVE)
*Portrait of Samuel Pepys (1633-1703), by John Riley (1646-1691), unknown date.*

FIG 27 (BELOW)
*Plaque marking the site of Samuel Pepys' house on Buckingham Street.*

barged through the outer purlieus of the city without any regard for the places or people that crossed their way. London seemed to have become a city of hoardings. The geometry of the lines left, according to a newspaper account,

*'shapeless scraps of land, unneeded by the railway, and unavailable for other purposes; wretched enclosures, where rubbish may be shot, broken crockery heaped, with the usual refuse of cabbage stalks, rusty, battered saucepans, dead animals, oyster-shells, and cast boots and shoes — odd ones, always, pairs never come together in these waste territories. Of the abominable bridges that cross the roads at ugly angles; of the viaducts that provide dry arches for the congregation and accommodation of street Arabs and gutter children; of the cucumber frames that supply light and air to the underground traffic; of the colossal sheds of stations, notably those that mar the river's banks, that soar and project, like Brobdignag poke-bonnets — we have no need to remind the reader. These are only to be classed as ruins, inasmuch as they are productive of and occasion ruins, and are themselves ruinous to all chance of the good-looking of London.'*

Near Charing Cross was the remains of 'a pneumatic railway tube passing' intended to pass under the river but never finished: an unsightly ruin, before so much as built.

Be this as it may, Hungerford Market provided as good a site for a station as could be found. On the edge of the river, it did not require the demolition of anything more than the market (on the north side of the Thames, that is). Admirers of Isambard Kingdom Brunel regretted the disappearance of the suspension bridge for foot passengers, serving the market, which he erected in the 1840s. It was removed to make way for a new railway bridge.

Although the site was fair, it cannot be said that Charing Cross Station has become one of the most fondly regarded of London termini. The Italianate station hotel designed by E. M. Barry fails to command the Strand. But the works brought one undoubted benefit:

'The summer of 1858 is remembered as the Great Stink, from the foul state of the sewage-infested River Thames.'

the Eleanor Cross which had been destroyed by the Puritans was erected in replica on the edge of the station forecourt. Charing Cross was once again Charing Cross in more than name.

Just as the Charing Cross Hotel was opening in 1865, another civil engineering project of epic proportions was underway. It began with Parliament holding its nose. The summer of 1858 is remembered as the Great

FIG 28
Detail from an Underground Electric Railways Company poster of 1914, by Charles Sharland, advertising the newly opened Charing Cross, Euston and Hampstead Railway extension to Charing Cross Underground station.

Stink, from the foul state of the sewage-infested River Thames. The nation's Parliamentarians, sitting on the edge of the river at Westminster, suffered along with the rest of the population, their windows being hung with curtains soaked in disinfecting chloride of lime. This was probably just as well; it brought home the need for action. The newly formed Metropolitan Board of Works (MBW) was charged with finding a remedy.

They already knew what had to be done. A number of Commissions had identified the problem of London's sewerage system, namely that much of it was discharged, untreated, into the Thames. Since the capital's drinking water was drawn from its river, cholera was a familiar evil, terrifying the rich as well as the poor. The degradation of the river was a relatively recent phenomenon. Fish had swum in the Thames until the 1820s. Until then, the conventional means of disposing of waste was by means of a cesspit dug under the house; this could be offensive to the occupants when it overflowed, and was hardly a joy to empty — though the contents had some value as manure. As the city grew, the price of manure necessarily fell, and the authorities allowed effluent to be drained into the streams and brooks that survived from the pre-urban landscape. These watercourses flowed into the Thames.

Joseph Bazalgette, the MBW's chief engineer, designed a new system, based around eighty-three miles of 'interceptory' sewers, running roughly parallel to the Thames, which would take sewage away to a safe distance to the east of the city. From the heights of Hampstead, the fall was sufficient to ensure a natural flow; but this was not the case in low lying areas such as Westminster or along the south bank. Here the flow was maintained by four great pumping stations at Pimlico, Deptford, Crossness (where the great beam engines can still be seen, handsomely restored) and the 'cathedral of sewage' Abbey Mills. In addition, over a thousand miles of street sewers were constructed. All the sewers were constructed of brick, and a visit on one of Thames Water's open days shows that, after more than a century of service, they have survived in remarkable condition, complete with their original pointing. The works included the construction of the Albert, Victoria and Chelsea Embankments, where sewers were built in conjunction with underground railway tunnels.

Today the Thames is once again home to over a hundred species of fish, though on stormy days small quantities of raw sewage still reach the Thames: an overflow provision which was acceptable in Bazalgette's day but which it is now hoped will be replaced. For the Northbank, a bonus, in terms of town planning, came in the shape of the Embankment, a plateau of previously non-existent land next to the river. Before the muddy foreshore of the Thames provided a ramshackle approach to the architecture above it. We have seen how both the Adams Brothers at the Adelphi and Sir William Chambers at Somerset House undertook embanking measures of their own. Now everyone could have the benefit of a spread of gardens, opened out beneath the Adelphi and the Savoy (its site still occupied by the ruins of a Tudor hospital), as well as a new thoroughfare to relieve the historic but congested artery of the Strand.

FIG 29
*Victoria Embankment Gardens — a verdant contrast to the sewage infested riverbank of earlier centuries.*

# Chapter Six

## *Serious Strand: The Law Courts*

The Law Courts killed George Edmund Street. That at least was the opinion of the architect's son, Arthur, who, in his memoir of his father, blamed Street's death, aged fifty-seven, in 1881 on the nervous strain and sheer labour entailed in the commission. It was an index of the impossible demands made both by the Gothic Revival in its heroic phase, and by the various government departments and commissions that concerned themselves with the design and execution of a great public work. Six of the courts Street provided were for Chancery, appropriately, since *Jarndyce v Jarndyce* itself hardly surpassed the building of the Royal Courts of Justice for frustration and bureaucratic delays.

In 1831 the founding of the Law Society had provided lawyers with a mouthpiece through which to urge for the courts (except criminal) to be concentrated on a single location. Previously, they had been divided between Westminster (Chancery) and Lincoln's Inn (common law) with the related chambers and offices scattered in between. A petition was presented to the House of Commons in 1841 and the next year Charles Barry, architect of the Houses of Parliament, designed a Greek Revival building to occupy Lincoln's Inn Fields. This site was quickly discarded but Barry had also suggested an alternative, an area of slums covering nearly eight acres north of the Strand that would provide a seven hundred foot frontage. To Sir Richard Bethell, a reforming lawyer and later Attorney General, it was 'a spit which...appears to have been created, and left, as it were, on purpose for this great improvement.'

During the 1850s the attractive idea of using the interest on the £1.3m lodged in Chancery, known as the Suitors' Fund, to finance the project was mooted; but reforms taking place in the law itself deferred the rebuilding of the courts. When Palmerston's administration returned to power in 1859, the pace — though never fast — somewhat quickened. A royal commission was appointed in 1860 and emphasised the 'daily mischief…fatigue, bodily ailment, dissatisfaction,' delay and cost caused by the existing arrangements.

The necessary money and site bills were passed — with opposition from 'economists' on the one hand, and advocates of a site on the Thames Embankment on the other — in 1865, and a Royal Courts of Justice Commission was appointed. This announced a competition for what was styled the Royal Palace of Justice. Few Victorian architects had much to say in favour of the competition system commonly used in the erection of public buildings, especially with the memory of Scott's debacle with Palmerston over the Foreign Office still fresh in mind. But the Law Courts competition was more mismanaged than most. The instructions, recalled Scott, were 'unprecedented in voluminousness, and the arrangements [which included speaking tubes, paper-chutes and lifts for large models that might be produced in court] were beyond all conception complicated and difficult.'

## '…Daily mischief… fatigue, bodily ailment, dissatisfaction, delay and cost…'

Eleven architects were invited to submit designs. When they did so all were in the Gothic style. At the time this was mistakenly thought to be a sign that the Gothic Revival had won the day as regards public architecture. Street's design was the best. It comprised a quadrangle of four ranges containing offices at the boundaries of the site, with a tall public hall, parallel to the Strand, rising from the centre. Around the hall were grouped the courts, twenty-three in number. The Strand elevation — in contrast to that finally built — was symmetrical in mass, although irregular in detail; while all sides sprouted the towers that were to be used as record depositories.

The judges were unable to decide and finally produced a verdict that pleased no one. They recommended that, since E.M.Barry (who produced a design not unlike his father's Houses of Parliament, but domed) had contrived the best plan, and Street's scheme had the best elevations, Barry and Street should be appointed joint architects. The other competitors, led by Waterhouse, objected vociferously, and the Attorney General, Sir John Karslake, consulted by the Treasury, said such an award would not be valid. Ultimately, on May 30, 1868, Street was appointed sole architect, although not declared the successful competitor. In a way that was suspect as well as unsatisfactory, Barry was awarded the consolation prize of victory in another, unrelated competition, for the new National Gallery, which was in the end never built.

But Street's troubles were far from over. The incoming Liberal administration insisted on a reduced scheme; and its first commissioner of works, Layard, was an enthusiast for the Thames Embankment site. The site question was a costly and time-consuming red herring. Street maintained — as he argued against Sir Charles Trevelyan before a committee appointed by the Society of Arts in March 1869 — that the Embankment site was narrower, less accessible and architecturally less appropriate than that chosen for the competition. Nevertheless, a Bill was laid before Parliament to acquire land from the Duke of Norfolk and others; and Street was required to redraw his scheme on a smaller scale for the new location.

In the end, considerations of economy prevailed. The Government already owned most of the Strand — or, as it was known, Carey Street — site, and on May 13, 1869, the first commissioner of works requested Street to prepare 'with as little delay as possible, a sketch showing how the reduced plan for the New Courts of Justice, as proposed to be erected on the Embankment site, can be adapted to the Carey Street site without any expenditure being incurred for purchasing additional land.'

The plans were ready by June 1; but with them Street sent an eleven-page letter of protest about the reductions. 'there can be no question that if ample open spaces for light and air and access are not indispensably required, and if there is not objection to placing public offices very high above ground, almost any amount of accommodation may be provided on any site,' he wrote sardonically. The competition site had been a regular rectangle, 560ft long by 500ft broad; the new site was smaller — 520ft by 475ft — and irregular. And Street spoke 'feelingly,' since he knew well 'where the responsibility will rest if this great building is not convenient.' The modifications necessary to meet the restrictions included turning the central hall through 90 degrees, to place it at right-angles to the Strand, its present position. Expenditure was limited first to £750,000, then to £710,000. But when the tenders for the superstructure of the building were received in 1872, the lowest from the Southampton firm of Joseph Bull and on, was for £719,787, using Chilmark Stone. With the addition of £20,000 for warming, £8,000 for gas lighting and £31,500 for the foundations already executed, Street calculated that the total would be £78,737 over the Treasury's figure. But since this included lunacy offices and some 'very useful spare rooms' not originally

FIG 30

*The Royal Courts of Justice. George Edmund Street was given the complex commission to design the new law courts in 1868, following a competition. They were not completed until 1882, after his death. One of the many changes forced on the architect during the project's lengthy gestation was the reorientation of the central hall, from a position parallel with the Strand to one at right angles to it. What had been a largely symmetrical composition ended by becoming irregular.*

FIG 31
*Cartoon of George Edmund Street, by Frederick Waddy (1848–1901),1873. Street's son thought the labour and anxiety of designing the Law Courts had killed him.*

specified, the real excess was considerably less. He pointed out that the Treasury had allowed Waterhouse a 15% increase for the Natural History Museum.

The Treasury's calculations were different and there began a long wrangle over assessments and estimates. The stone for the Law Courts had to be Portland. And the first commission of works strongly objected to Street's proposal to save money by using deal rather than wainscot for the joinery. Street pared more off the building. The two figures edged closer together but did not meet. The Treasury remained adamant.

The special object of criticism was precisely the feature that made Street's design distinctive and had remained constant throughout the vicissitudes, namely the central hall. Aesthetic criticism in the press had not been wanting — 'a gloomy vault,' James Fergusson called it in Macmillan's Magazine. Street responded with a pamphlet. To the Treasury the central hall merely seemed a gross extravagance. The nadir of Street's relations with the officials was reached in April 1873 when it was suggested that a considerable saving — £80,000 — could be made by omitting the roof and pinnacles of the central hall, and providing shelter from inclement weather by means of cloisters. Negotiations broke down altogether on June

6, when Street declared himself 'quite unable to make the reductions required by the First Commissioner of Works in the cost of the Building.'

The Treasury was forced to give in. 'The question has recently engaged the attention of HM's Government,' wrote the Lords Commissioners on July 1, and Street's plans were approved. But they were plans from which, by a long process of attrition, every penny of not strictly necessary expenditure had been worn away. As is the way of such things, not all the economies were well advised. Much of the anxiety that hastened Street's death was caused by the employment of an inexperienced contractor who had cut his tender to the bone. A strike of stonemasons in 1877 made it necessary to employ French, German and Italian workmen from September 24 to December that year.

Yet paradoxically Street's design did in some respects benefit from the modifications he resisted. Street fought hard to have a symmetrical plan but today it is the boldly varied and broken outline, with, from the west, the succession of gables, turrets and pinnacles that ends emphatically in the great clock tower that seems the design's greatest strength. The full length of the front can be seen only obliquely; economy forced a solution that suits the English taste for the Picturesque, somewhat in the style of the Grecian National Gallery. It may also be that the repeated need to concentrate and strip down the design gave Street's already taut and vigorous style an added tension. The greatest regret must be that, although a more lenient administration allowed Street £4,527 1s 10d over contract in 1881, the carving executed under Thomas Earp was restricted to some 70% of that intended.

'Mr Justice Darling was forced to use a temporary court in the form of a wooden hut erected within the central hall.'

Inside, the principal feature remained the central hall. Vaulted in stone like a cathedral, it is one of the great extravagances of the Gothic Revival — a vast and majestic passageway between courts. At 230ft in length, it is little shorter (although much narrower) than Westminster Hall, longer than the Wladislawschen Saal in Prague, or the Salle des pas Perdus, in Paris. Altogether there are seven hundred and fifty rooms.

On Street's death, the building was finished by his son, Arthur, in conjunction with

A C Blomfield. A memorial with a seated figure by H H Armstead was erected at the east side of the central hall in 1882. And Street's stand against reductions was vindicated within two decades of his death, since by 1900 there had already been calls for more courts to be built. Mr Justice Darling was forced to use a temporary court in the form of a wooden hut erected within the central hall.

Action was taken by the Office of Works in 1908 when the Law Courts were extended to the west in a style sympathetic to Street's building. Was this the final acknowledgement of Street's genius which previous administrations had done so much to frustrate? If so it came too late and typically went awry. An outcry was caused because the new building occupied an open space laid out as a garden, and the architect Leonard Stokes wrote to *The Times* complaining that the plans were 'a sort of *rechauffé* of Street.'

FIG 32
*The great hall at the Royal Courts of Justice. Essentially a cathedral-like circulation space, the great hall was Street's great architectural indulgence, to which he clung through the many cost-saving exercises imposed on him by successive governments.*

# Chapter Seven

## *Playful Strand: Shopping, Hotels and Theatres*

Nowadays, it may seem that G E Street's Royal Courts of Justice, decked in all the cathedral-like solemnity of the Gothic Revival, were a typical product of their age. When they were built, however, their cliff-like façades must have appeared more like an atoll, standing proudly but in isolation above a sea of dereliction and vice. One slum may have been cleared to provide the site on which they were built, but others stood round about. With poverty went vice. Charing Cross, Covent Garden, Fleet Street and the Strand had long been synonymous with prostitution.

Figure 33 shows the burning of the notorious Star Tavern in the Strand, fired, along with two other bawdy houses, by sailors from Wapping who had been fleeced there. Hedge Lane near Charing Cross may have had as many as twenty brothels in it. Prostitutes, working in pairs, often robbed their clients, some of whom were lucky to get away with their lives. Otherwise their rewards were meagre: the sheer number of prostitutes — some of whom were no more than children — drove down the price that they could extract from their clients. All manner of sexual proclivity was catered for. The bundle of birch rods on the wall above the Harlot's bed in Plate 3 of Hogarth's *A Harlot's Progress* hints at one taste. A veil of fantasy was drawn over the sordidness of the transaction by the Folly, a floating brothel anchored in the Thames opposite Somerset House, where musicians serenaded 'water-nymphs' and 'tritons;' trysts took place in small apartments on the floor above.

The authorities should have tackled the

FIG 33
*The Tar's Triumph, or Bawdy House Battery, etching by Charles Mosley, 1749. The Star Tavern and two other bawdy houses were burnt down by sailors from Wapping who had been fleeced in them.*

problem at the root and charged the brothel-keepers; an indication of how difficult this could be was given when two constables and their assistants were driven out of Eagle Court, off the Strand, by a gang of thirty bullies or pimps. It was easier to bring the prostitutes themselves to book, although it is doubtful that this did much to decrease supply. A common punishment for a prostitute was to be whipped while walking behind a cart the length of the Strand, from Charing Cross to Somerset House. Presumably this indicated a likely scene of her activities. Brothels were often made out of houses which fell into dereliction at the end of their leases, when the tenant had little incentive to maintain them. The Strand area would remain plagued by slums until the dawn of the twentieth century. The number of prostitutes remained high.

Their activities had long been associated

10788. - LONDON. THAMES EMBANKMENT.

FIG 34

*The hotels Cecil and Savoy, from a postcard printed circa 1900. Richard D'Oyly Carte opened the Savoy Theatre in 1881; trips to the United States to protect copyrights introduced him to the luxury hotels there, and in 1889 he opened the Savoy Hotel. To attract guests to what had been a raffish area, he employed the Swiss hotelier César Ritz to run the establishment and Auguste Escoffier to preside over the kitchen. The Savoy was followed by the Hotel Cecil, the biggest in Europe when it was opened in 1896.*

with the theatre. Until the building of Shaftesbury Avenue, finished in 1886, and other West End improvements at the end of the nineteenth century, London's Theatreland was located around the Strand. The street is supposed to have had more theatres and music halls than any other in London — which was saying something, because their numbers had boomed everywhere since the removal of restrictions by the Theatre Act of 1843. Only a few theatres — such as the St James's, the Haymarket, the Criterion in Piccadilly and the Princess's in Oxford Street — were any distance from it. The offering ranged from the high art of Henry Irving at the Lyceum to farce, melodrama and variety shows at the Gaiety and the Olympic — neither of the last two being better than they should be, in the opinion of the London County Council, which inspected them as part of its campaign against prostitution in the 1890s. (Inspectors actually closed the Empire Music Hall in Leicester Square, with its notorious promenade behind the dress circle, provoking an outcry by the cabbies and local tradespeople whose business needed the crowds of theatregoers who flocked there.)

Many theatres remain — the Vaudeville, the Adelphi, the Novello and others. But nostalgic thespians cannot help but lament the ravages made by the modern world. Let our guide, in this respect, be W Macqueen Pope who imagined an elderly theatre goer looking for vanished haunts among the Strand of 1951:

*He can still see Terry's Theatre, over which a vast modern store has flowed, the old Tivoli before it surrendered to a cinema, the front of the old Adelphi with its canopy right across the street... Maybe he can remember the original Gaiety and perhaps Toole's, long since swept away. The old Strand Theatre has gone, its site is a tube station... there is not a sign of the old Globe, the Olympic or the Opera Comique, all of which adjoined the Strand and have passed into shadows with Newcastle Street, Holywell Street, Wych Street, almost medieval thoroughfares in appearance. Vast modern sarcophagi cover them all. The Vaudeville is still there, modernised inside, and so is the Adelphi, modernised throughout...*

Then came 'a name and a building' that were:

*...the very pulse and mainspring of the Strand when the Strand was the Street of Professionals-of Theatre and Music Hall alike and still, over a little canopy, some copper cupids dance — it is a funeral rite now, but once it was the welcome to as gay a place as any city in the world could show-a restaurant of strong character and complete distinction — that entirely delectable place known as Romano's.*

FIG 35
*César Ritz, known as the King of Hoteliers, and the Hotelier to Kings.*

Romano's had not been what it was since 1914. In its heyday, the heady mixture of actors, authors, journalists, artists, lawyers, financiers, prize fighters, army officers, gentlemen, cads and crooks created a club-like atmosphere, Bohemian in spirit and as golden as the currency then in circulation. The spirit of Romano's was the spirit of the Strand.

# The Savoy Theatre and Hotel

The Strand had, in the 1870s and 1880s, been rather too Bohemian for polite society. That its character became more respectable, while still being interestingly raffish, was largely due to the Savoy Hotel.

It began with the Savoy Theatre. This was the creation of Richard D'Oyly Carte, the son of a musician from Berners Street in Soho. He had something of a family connection with the Savoy, since his grandfather had been vicar of the Savoy Chapel — a royal peculiar, or private chapel of the King, in his right as Duke of Lancaster; it had been built by Henry VII to serve the hospital which replaced John of Gaunt's palace and is the only ancient building to survive from the site. Carte entered the family musical business, as well as writing his own songs and operettas. But his real strength was as an impresario. In 1875 he fitted W.S.Gilbert and Arthur Sullivan's *Trial by Jury* into an evening at the Royalty Theatre otherwise occupied by a piece by Offenbach. Its brilliant reception led him to organise a syndicate which staged *HMS Pinafore*, which ran for seven hundred nights; but the syndicate collapsed amid acrimony and Carte founded his own company, which thereafter presented all the works of G and S, initially at the Opéra Comique on the Strand. The money rolled in; *The Pirates of Penzance* (1880) was quickly followed by *Patience* (1880); and the Opéra Comique soon proved too small for the audiences. It was time for Carte to invest his

FIG 36
*The entrance to the Savoy.*

*The Jazz Age awning in stainless steel was designed by Sir Howard Robertson in 1929. Earlier in the 1920s, the Savoy Theatre had been given glamorous Art Deco interiors by Basil Ionides.*

profits in a scruffy corner of land that had once been part of the Savoy Palace. Opened in 1881, the Savoy Theatre was the most sophisticated of its age, claiming to be the first public building in the world lit entirely by electricity. That was a gamble, and Carte had to demonstrate its safety by breaking a light bulb on stage to show that it did not prove an imminent fire risk. Patrons were right to be concerned; theatres often burnt down, sometimes with loss of life.

Electricity would, of course, prove far safer than gas, but women still feared that the glaring light levels associated with electricity might not be flattering to their complexions.

Electricity was not the only innovation at the Savoy. Carte gave the audience free programmes. The crowd entering the pit and gallery was expected to form an orderly queue. The proscenium curtain was not painted but made of luxurious quilted silk. Gilbert and

# Strand Restaurants

A swirling cartouche in terracotta at the entrance to Savoy Buildings commemorates the Fountain Tavern that once stood nearby. It was one of many resorts of conviviality associated with the Strand. In the early eighteenth century, the Fountain was practically an extension of Parliament for the Tory peers and MPs – nearly as many as three hundred at a time – who met there to thrash out strategy. It was succeeded by the Unicorn, which became the Coal Hole, before collapsing when the foundations of Terry's Theatre were dug in 1887.

Memories of dinners eaten, many of them raffish, linger ghost-like about the Strand. At the beginning of the twentieth century, Romano's was as close, in atmosphere, as London got to being Paris: champagne really was drunk out of the dainty slippers of girls from the Gaiety theatre. It had been begun by the eponymous Romano, head waiter at the Café Royal. Beginning in a small way as the Café Vaudeville, it grew under the patronage of *The Sporting Times* (universally known as *The Pink 'Un*) and the Leamar Sisters, a music hall act who sang about it as

> Romano's, Italiano
> Paradise in the Strand . . .

Decorated in the fashionable Byzantine style, the restaurant attracted a theatrical crowd, among whom moved high spirited army officers. Edward VII himself loved it.

Restasurants close, others open, but one has endured the caprices of fashion to be as popular today as it has been for approaching two centuries: Simpsons-in-the-Strand. It opened in 1828 as the Grand Cigar Divan, a coffee house when customers could play chess. Victorians like Sherlock Holmes, who dined there twice with Watson, might not recognise the *décor*, since the Cigar Divan was remodelled – and renamed – in 1903-4. But the panelled walls and coffered ceiling, the starched white table cloths echoed by the long aprons of the waiters, remain unaltered.  Joints of beef are still wheeled to the table beneath domed trolleys. Simpson's was an institution when Miss Wilcox invited Margaret to luncheon there in *Howard's End*. It remains an institution, as near to immortality as an eating house can achieve.

*Images, clockwise from top left: Menu from Romano's Restaurant, circa 1896; Cartoon by H M Bateman, advertising Simpson's in the Strand; Woodcut of a show taking place at the Coal Hole, circa 1854; The plaque that marks the former location of the Fountain Tavern.*

The gentleman who asked the carver whether the meat was English or Foreign.

Sullivan's works were soon known as the Savoy operas.

To protect copyrights and mount his own transatlantic productions, Carte visited the United States. There he was impressed by a new style of building: the luxury hotel. It was unfamiliar to London. Carte determined to build one next to this theatre. The Strand, still a narrow as well as disreputable street, was a far from obvious location, as can be seen from the decision to put the entrance on the river front, where carriages could draw up in a large courtyard; no risk that patrons would have to push their way past creatures of the night. Indeed, the building tried, as far as possible, to ignore the Strand, preferring to look out over

FIG 41
*The Corinthia Hotel.*

*Originally the Hotel Metropole, it stands on Northumberland Avenue, built in 1884. In 1896, a motorcar rally had left from it, heading for the south coast: the first of the London to Brighton runs.*

the Thames, making the most of the views. Like the theatre, the hotel was to be modern; hydraulic lifts were provided by the American Elevation Company. It was also irresistible. To run the establishment, Carte brought over César Ritz, who stayed for eight years; the most famous chef in the world, Auguste Escoffier, presided over the kitchen. The combination successfully appealed to an age adapting itself to hitherto unknown standards of plutocratic luxury. The extreme starchiness of Victorian social conventions was softening. Previously, respectable ladies had only dined in their own and their friends' houses. Carte made it possible for them to eat at the Savoy.

Queen Victoria died in 1901, and so did Richard D'Oyly Carte. Britain stood at the beginning of a new century and a new age. The Savoy Hotel had spawned imitators. Next to it was the Hotel Cecil, the façade of which survives; with over eight hundred rooms it was the largest hotel in Europe when it opened in 1896 . Not far away, on Northumberland Avenue — a new road that, in 1884, had ploughed through the old town palace of the Dukes of Northumberland — was the Metropole (reopened as the Corinthia in 2011). In 1896, a motorcar rally had left from it, heading for the south coast: the first of the London to Brighton runs. Change was afoot, not least

for the Northbank. Theatres and prostitutes were moving west. The Strand was about to be widened, new streets would soon be created, and the pestilential, vice-ridden courts and alleyways where the poor had lived for two centuries cleared away. In 1853, Charlotte Brontë described the heroine of *Villette* exploring London:

*Descending, I went wandering whither chance might lead, in a still ecstasy of freedom and enjoyment; and I got — I know not how — I got into the heart of city life. I saw and felt London at last: I got into the Strand...*

There was a real frisson of danger to it. By the time Elizabeth followed her footsteps in Virginia Woolf's *Mrs Dalloway*, 1925, the vibrancy remained, but there was little to fear.

'Let's all go down The Strand,' went an Edwardian song:

> *Oh what a happy land*
> *That's the place for fun and noise*
> *All among the girls and boys*
> *So let's all go down The Strand.*

Northbank had become safe.

# Chapter Eight

## *Crown Imperial: The Strand Improvement Scheme and the Queen Victoria Memorial*

It is a June morning in 1911. The time is exactly 10.25am. Rain has been falling on and off, but fortunately the golden, preposterously fairytale State coach, made in the mid-eighteenth century, is closed. Fanfares sound, the National Anthem plays, and George V and Queen Mary emerge from Buckingham Palace. Eight horses take the strain of the coach and it rumbles across the forecourt, past two hundred cheering Chelsea Pensioners, to join the coronation procession.

Another King, George V's father, Edward VII, had made the same journey to Westminster Abbey a decade before, when he was crowned. Few details of the scene had changed since then. Guardsmen in bearskins stand at the salute. Detachments of troops have been sent from India, the Dominions and the Colonies. With European royalties, many of them related to the King, being ferried in no fewer than twenty-four State Landaus, the front of the procession arrives an hour before the end of it sets off. George V is a highly conservative man. But he does permit one innovation. On its way to the Abbey, the procession does not turn abruptly left, to go through Horse Guards' Parade. Instead, it sweeps smoothly onwards, through the central of the three mighty arches that piece the sweeping Baroque façade of Admiralty Arch. It has just been finished. There was some doubt, earlier in the year, that it would be ready in time: the London County Council was squabbling with the Office of Works about who should pay to remove some obstructions on the farther side. Unlike the rest of the soot-grimed capital, the freshly erected Portland stone is still cream-coloured and pristine. This is the first time that it has been used.

As an addition to the ceremonial route, Admiralty Arch must have been particularly gratifying to George V. Like his great-granduncle William IV, he was a sailor king. Purists may have criticised the structure for combining a piece of monumental scenery with civil service accommodation — an expedient that allowed the cost of construction to fall on the Admiralty, rather than the Office of Works. But there was also a symbolic fitness to the arrangement. The British navy was the most powerful in the world. It absorbed a fifth of all government expenditure. A quarter of a million people worked for or in the Service. 'The Admiralty built and maintained an enormous fleet,'

'The Admiralty specified, designed and often manufactured every variety of stores from chamber-pots to torpedoes...'

wrote N A M Rodger in *The Admiralty*, 1979, 'it specified, designed and often manufactured every variety of stores from chamber-pots to torpedoes. It fed, clothed and supervised its officers and men from boyhood to the grave, and to a considerable extent their wives and children with them.' The British Empire rested on the shoulders of its seamen. Admiralty Arch was part of an imperial conception of urban improvements that would render London more worthy of its position as the capital of a great Empire. Its intimate connection with British seapower could not have been more apt.

Admiralty Arch formed part of the Queen Victoria Memorial conceived to honour the Queen-Empress by providing a proper setting for the state and panoply of monarchy in the motorcar age. Within a month of her death in 1901, a Committee for the Memorial had been formed, under the chairmanship of the Prime Minister, Lord Salisbury. The new monarch, cosmopolitan Edward VII, particularly wanted it to be architectural in character. The result included a towering monument to the late Queen, sculpted by Thomas Brock (whose profile of her already graced the coinage) and, in 1913, a new façade for Buckingham Palace, designed in a distinctly French style by Sir Aston Webb. But like Admiralty Arch, these were only incidents in one of the few examples of grand Classical town planning ever achieved in London. Debouching via a new entrance into Trafalgar Square, it led not only to Whitehall and Westminster Abbey but linked with the Strand Improvement Scheme and Aldwych to form a new route to the City of London. An imperial route. Eventually, all the High Commissions of the most important British Empire and Dominions would adorn it — Canada, South Africa, Australia and India.

Unlike Paris, Rome or Madrid, London is not a planned city: it grew organically, absorbing pre-existing villages as private landlords developed their estates. The great nineteenth century planner had been John Nash; but his achievement in building Regent Street for the Office of Woods and Forests had been the combination of pragmatism and Picturesque theory which allowed him to follow a line that kinked, bent and sidestepped — changes that he ingeniously concealed through the clever placing of round churches and quadrants. There was no autocracy in Britain capable of driving through the avenues and boulevards, their views terminating in a distant monument, such as Baron Haussmann bestowed on Paris. Yet London was the capital of the greatest Empire that the world had ever seen. Edward VII, who initiated the Mall scheme, was a particular admirer of Paris, a city that he associated not only with good living

'The king seized a sword and knighted the sculptor on the spot.'

and the sins of the flesh but the triumphs of the Ecole des Beaux-Arts.

The theme of the Victoria Memorial was set in the monument outside Buckingham Palace. Gruff and choleric, George V — a home-loving man, who liked stamp collecting and uniforms — was not famous for his aesthetic taste. But he responded so warmly to Brock's work that, in an uncharacteristically impromptu act, he seized a sword and knighted the sculptor on the spot. Brock was the sort of artist the King could do business with. An excellent shot, he loved rowing and served as a volunteer with the Artists' Rifles. Apart from the smock that he wore over spongebag trousers, he looks as much like a bank manager as an artist. But his imagination rose to the challenge of the Memorial, heavy both with Aberdeen granite (sixteen hundred tons of it form the steps and pavement) and symbolism. Beside the huge figure of Queen Victoria sit Truth and Charity, while another golden angel — who can be variously interpreted as Peace or Victory — hovers above. Because the British Empire depended on the might of the Royal Navy and British dominance in shipping, the iconography is strongly nautical; mermaids and mermen sport with hippogriffs.

The art magazine *The Studio* acclaimed the result:

'At last we may congratulate ourselves that we have, in the centre of London town, a sculptural monument of supreme importance which British art may claim with pride...In its unity, dignity, and nobility of conception, its large simplicity and harmonious beauty of design, and its accordance with the great vital ideals of sculpture in the true structural expressiveness and the broad live modelling of natural form, [it] is in every way worthy of its purpose as a national and imperial tribute.'

But the tribute had only just begun; it was to continue in the reconfiguration of the Mall, Admiralty Arch and the junction of the Mall with Trafalgar Square. Those works fell to the prolific and highly organised Sir Aston Webb.

The anonymous author of Webb's *Times* obituary in 1930 considered that it was 'doubtful' that he was a great architect. 'The fact is that he was almost too successful. His work was so vast that he had to surround himself with clerks — people say, 50 at least — so that his office became more like a Government Department than the studio of a man who had time to think and draw.' But he was a man of supreme organisational ability — demonstrated by the remodelling of Buckingham Palace that took place in 1913. On August 5, the royal family left for Balmoral; a mere thirteen weeks later it was ready for their reoccupation

FIG 42
*Sir Thomas Brock in his studio, photograph by Ralph Winwood Robinson, 1889.*

*Brock's later career was dominated by the construction of the Victoria Memorial outside Buckingham Palace. George V was so delighted by the result that he knighted Brock on the spot.*

FIG 43

*Admiralty Arch, built as part of the scheme to remodel the Mall, in memory of Queen Victoria. Although a triumphal arch, it incorporated offices and apartments for the Admiralty – an example of official parsimony which also emphasised the importance of British sea power. Few other architects than Sir Aston Webb, a man of supreme organisational ability, could have persuaded government ministers to build it.*

when the scaffolding came down on October 31. Dealing with Government Departments and royal households requires different skills from that of the purely art architect. Ministers respected his capabilities. Few architects other than Webb could have convinced them to go so far beyond the original brief for the Victoria Memorial, persuading them to create a new ceremonial route which would lead from Buckingham Palace to Trafalgar Square, until then inaccessible from The Mall. As the architect H V Lanchester commented, Webb was a 'born leader of men' who 'possessed the happy gift of seeing not only the right course to pursue but also the best method of convincing others of the soundness of his opinions'. Those qualities were crucial to the success of the Victoria Memorial.

Opening The Mall into Trafalgar Square was a masterstroke. One of the triumphs of Admiralty Arch is that it enables an awkward change of direction to be carried out seamlessly, without people travelling the route being aware of it.

From Trafalgar Square, traffic, royal or otherwise, could roll eastwards to the City of London, along streets that had been widened or newly built in the Strand Improvement Scheme, Aldwych and Kingsway. Long in planning, bitterly fought in execution, they nevertheless provided London with a new vision, in which

the desire for imperial scale in a better planned city combined with urgent need to clear foetid slums.

## The Aldwych and Kingsway

One of the first acts of the London County Council when it was established in 1889 was to publish a Bill 'to widen and improve the Strand.' Perhaps there was still ringing in their ears Charles Dickens Jr's criticism that 'at present there is no street of equal importance in any capital of Europe so unworthy of its position.' To Dickens Jr, the Strand was cramped, its course obstructed by the churches of St Clement Danes and St Mary le Strand, both of which he would have swept away. The LCC would also have done evil to the churches, if not prevented by a campaign led by the artist Walter Crane. However, more objectionable even than churches blocking traffic were the notorious 'rookeries' of decaying courts and alleys. They proposed not only to widen the Strand itself but to create a dazzling, electrically lit boulevard in Kingsway, shooting like an arrow northwards from the curved bow of another new thoroughfare, Aldwych. The idea of a new north-south road, connecting Holborn with the Strand, had been mooted as long ago as the 1830s. Aldwych and Kingsway not only provided that artery but, slicing mercilessly through the existing pattern of streets, purged London of one of the worst of its remaining slums.

These days, historians would surely deplore the clearing of Clare Market. West of Covent Garden, it was, architecturally, an example of what the City of London had been like before the Great Fire. But the Elizabethan buildings had degenerated into squalor, where the presence of a market famous for selling tripe 'stale and revolting-looking portions of the internal parts of animals, or foul-smelling remnants of inferior joints, cooked or uncooked,' did nothing to improve the amenity.

Photographs, though, do not suggest that the area was — as far as the buildings went — quite as tumbledown as reformers complained. Even before Clare Market was demolished, the *Standard* fell victim to nostalgia, publishing a lament for the disappearance of the market, whose impoverished streets had become the architectural equivalent of the living dead:

*'At the doors of these decaying tenements which are not closed and untenanted, gaunt, poverty-stricken women crouch, and children huddle. There are no vehicles passing through the streets. Men stand about at the door of the casual ward hard by, many of them with a furtive, deprecatory look, and bearing in their worn faces the marks of disappointment and hunger, and a sense of the general wrongness of things, but without interchanging more than the occasional muttered word or two expressive of weary, but patient waiting for the opening of the door. The dark shed-like building at an opposite corner is, as one may see, the parish soup kitchen, and two short streets off is the mission hall, where at the moment, this being time for the evening service, there is a sound of singing, which comes with pathetic suggestion, from a few voices of women and children; but there is scarcely any other sound. The men — many of them in the lowest stage of poverty — who hang about the streets, already look like evicted tenants. The district, where no prevailing industry seems to have survived, bears the signs of being doomed: the houses here and there have, something of the look of the old abodes that are still to be seen about Gough-square and Bolt-court — genteel houses with outside shutters, and the shabby remains of what was once acknowledged respectability — but they are like dwellings avoided because their inmates have been smitten by the plague. Indeed, this district of Clare Market suggests what a London neighbourhood must have been when each house-front had been marked with a cross, and the few surviving tenants crept out, silent and desponding, to breathe in greater freedom the already tainted air.'*

# The London School of Economics

The symbolic centre of Empire, Northbank was also brewing ideas that the King Emperor would have been less than comfortable with. In 1895, Beatrice and Sidney Webb, Graham Wallas and George Bernard Shaw met at a breakfast party in Surrey. The year before, the Fabian Society, of which they were the leading members, had received a bequest of £20,000. They now decided to use this money to found a School which would study the problems of poverty and analyse inequalities of wealth, for the betterment of society. It should be a movement as much as an institution, 'a centre not only of lectures on special subjects,' as Beatrice Webb observed in her diary, 'but an association of students who would be directed and supported in doing original work.' The London School of Economics was born.

The founders chose rooms for it off the Strand, an area closely associated with the sort of social evils they wished to abolish. That October the first classes were held in rooms in John Street, in the Adelphi. A year later, the LSE moved to 10 Adelphi Terrace. When the LCC cleared Clare market, it provided the LSE with its present site, off Aldwych. To do justice to George V, he laid the foundation stone of the Old Building in 1920.

Like King's College, the LSE now occupies several sites around Northbank, including the New Academic Building — 'jaw-dropping,' according to the Independent — designed by Nicholas Grimshaw and opened in 2008. The £71m structure comprises four lecture theatres, sixteen seminar rooms, a street café and a rooftop pavilion that is one of the best places from which to enjoy the roofscape of Northbank.

FIG 44
*The old entrance to the LSE's
Old Building, circa 1940.*

A report of the LCC's Housing of the Working Classes Committee of 1895 saw it as 'the largest and worst of those crowded collections of the courts and alleys to disgrace central London.'

Property owners had not welcomed the Strand Improvement Scheme. One had written to *The Times*, as soon as the Bill was published, declaring that 'its effect will be to create open war, and war to the knife, between the Council' and the people who owned, or lived in, affected buildings. The issue was how the scheme was to be paid for. The Council, however, was both determined and pragmatic. It took ten years of negotiation before their bill could be passed, but passed it was in 1899; the next summer, workmen began to demolish the rookery of Clare Market. Five years later, *The Times* gasped at the transformation that had been wrought: 'Lofty buildings and time-honoured land-marks have been swept away, whole streets demolished, and the face of London in this locality completely transformed.' No fewer than fifty-one public houses were closed. The Strand was widened. St Mary le Strand and St Clement Danes became islands in the middle of the street, the latter losing its churchyard.

When Edward VII arrived to open the new road on October 18, 1905, the sun shone brightly throughout the day; the perfect weather was taken to be a good omen for the development.

As yet, the site was largely empty of buildings. Construction, however, was, or would soon be, underway. The corner of the Strand and Aldwych was already graced by Richard Norman Shaw's New Gaiety Theatre, crowned by a dome and allegorical figure (alas, demolished in 1957); opposite the Morning Post building, Inveresk House, designed by Mewès and Davis of the Ritz Hotel, would arise in 1907. The Waldorf Hotel, backed by the millionaire William Waldorf Astor, went up at the same time, its wide façade, designed by Alexander Mackenzie, fronted by giant Ionic pilasters stretching through three floors. The mood is expansive, self-confident. Africa House on Kingsway bears a sculptural composition by Benjamin Clemens, featuring a big game hunter and dead elephants, among other now politically incorrect figures. Elsewhere, pairs of figures flank escutcheons bearing the monogram IB — Imperial Building.

> 'Lofty buildings and time-honoured land-marks have been swept away, whole streets demolished, and the face of London in this locality completely transformed.'

FIG 45

*In 1913, work began on Australia House, on a site that had become, to some eyes, a garden of wild flowers. It continued through the First World War, being officially opened by George V in 1918. Housing the oldest Australian diplomatic mission and the longest continuously occupied foreign mission in London, the High Commission symbolises the strength of feeling that had reinforced between the two countries by the First World War.*

Their attributes — hammers, ocean lines, armour, quill pen — symbolise work, commerce, military might and learning. As with the Queen Victoria Memorial, the note was imperial — but also modern. Behind their stone-cladding, these tall blocks were built on steel frames, and they were serviced by hot water and electric lifts. Kingsway was the only London boulevard to have a tramway running beneath it.

In 1913, work began on Australia House, on a site that had become, to some eyes, a garden of wild flowers. It continued through the First World War, being officially opened in 1918 by George V. Housing the oldest Australian diplomatic mission and the longest continuously occupied foreign mission in London, the High Commission symbolises the strength of feeling that was reinforced between the two countries by the First World War.

Unity between the English speaking peoples was also the theme chosen by Irving T. Bush. An American, he intended Bush House — designed by the American architect Harvey Wiley Corbett — to act as a vast trade centre. This did not prove successful, but the building's giant exedra gave Kingsway a spectacular southern termination: above a screen of Ionic columns, two heroic figures clasp hands in an epic gesture of Anglo-American friendship. Later Bush House became famous as the home of the BBC World Service.

In July 1930, the King returned to Aldwych to open India House. The architect, Sir Herbert Baker, has been reviled for his unhelpful attitude towards Lutyens at New Delhi and his desecration of Sir John Soane's Bank of England, which Baker enlarged and remodelled. But his Arts and Crafts aesthetic responded to the challenge of a building that in some sense expressed the spirit of India. The exterior, of an almost dazzling whiteness when it was unveiled, is marked by restrained decorative passages — slender pillars surmounted by seated lions sculptured in stone; a crown and a star; a carved frieze; and coloured and gilded plaques.

As George V's carriage rolled out of Buckingham Palace, proceeded beneath Admiralty Arch and swept past Herbert Baker's South Africa House, before making its stately way along the Strand to Australia House and India House in the Aldwych, the King may well have felt that the finishing touch had, after three decades, been put on London as the capital of the British Empire.

FIG 46
*South Africa House, built by the Arts and Crafts-inspired Herbert Baker, who had built many government buildings and country houses in South Africa. It is one of several imperial buildings on the route between Buckingham Palace and Aldwych, improved in the early twentieth century.*

FIG 47
*A view in Aldwych, with Herbert Baker's India House on the left.*

# Chapter Nine
## Art Deco and Post War

Maroons burst over London. From his office in the Ministry of Munitions, Winston Churchill looked out over Trafalgar Square. It was filling up with people. Agitated people. Happy, noisy people. People so excited that they were in danger of displays of emotion quite alien to the national stereotype of repressed self-control. The pigeons took to the air and flocked around Nelson's column. Below them, those humans who could hurried on, towards Buckingham Palace. But the Mall was soon full. So they climbed Landseer's lions, they danced, they scaled the lampposts, they clambered onto taxis, clinging to the roof and sides. Flag-sellers appeared, as though from nowhere; before long everybody had a flag. A cornet played 'Auld Lang Syne'. An attempt to sing the *Marseillaise* was not successful. Nobody minded. It was November 11, 1918, and the Armistice had been signed.

As so often at moments of national drama or rejoicing, Trafalgar Square was the place to be. An overflowing tide of humanity filled it, like a lake. Hope was in the air. Exhausted and impoverished by four years of war, Britain would change. It had to. Over the next half century, Northbank would exemplify the ways in which it did so. Not all of it was for the better although it can be said that campaigners succeeded in avoiding the worst.

In 1922, the Arts and Crafts architect Ernest Newton — whose country house practice had, like his health, been ruined by the war, which, as president of the Royal Institute of British Architects, he spent issuing building licences — took stock of the Strand. It contained 'more old buildings than any other large thoroughfare in London... in traversing the Strand one could see several seventeenth-century houses still existing.' The Adelphi had barely changed since the Adam brothers finished it. Today, as we have seen, Buckingham Street survives from the

1670s and fragments of the Adelphi remain; but a century of commercial development has taken its toll. There are now no seventeenth-century houses in the Strand. The scale has changed.

The process had begun in the Edwardian period. Until 1906, the British Medical Association, for example, occupied various structures on a corner site on the Strand and Agar Street. That year, however, the doctors held a competition for a headquarters that would express their authority and status more adequately; they had evolved from the Provincial Medical and Surgical Association to become a powerful professional body, capable, within a few years, of altering Lloyd George's Act for providing workers with state medical attention. The architect, Charles Holden, would become familiar to commuters for the underground stations that he designed, under the patronage of Frank Pick, the Maecenas of London Transport. In contrast to Norman Shaw's Baroque and Mewès and Davis's dix-huitième at the other end of the Strand, Holden's design was Mannerist. It used elements of Classicism but in a new way. London had become used to liberties being taken with the classical vocabulary since the emergence of architects like Charles Harrison Townsend, practising an Art Nouveauish Free Style. Holden's distinctly staccato building was more rigorous. It had little surface charm. Windows with sculptural figures squashed into panels, reminiscent of Michelangelo, were combined with an almost manic vertical emphasis, created by pilasters of different heights. The sculptures were provided by twenty-six year old Jacob Epstein who had studied in Paris. The theme was to be, loosely, *The Seven Ages of Man*. The BMA wanted the figures to represent eminent doctors, but, as Epstein recalled, 'I was determined to do a series of nude figures, and surgeons with side-whiskers, no matter how eminent, could hardly have served my purpose as models.' Architect and sculptor had their way, and eighteen nudes were carved out of single blocks of stone, in situ. They were stylised but anatomically frank; the figure of Maternity, for example, was shown as pregnant. Fig leaves were dispensed with. By a quirk of fate, the

'Windows with sculptural figures squashed into panels, reminiscent of Michelangelo, were combined with an almost manic vertical emphasis, created by pilasters of different heights.'

building on the opposite side of Agar Street housed the National Vigilance Association; they were certainly vigilant enough to spot what was happening outside their own windows. A brewing storm burst in the Evening Standard in 1908. 'BOLD SCULPTURE, AMAZING FIGURES ON A STRAND BUILDING,' proclaimed a seemingly innocuous headline, before asking: 'BUT IS IT ART?' In fact the author was less concerned about the art question than the corruption of public morals. 'They are a form of statuary which no careful father would want his daughter, or no discriminating young man his fiancée, to see.' When eleven years after the BMA left for large premises in Tavistock Square in 1924, the building's new owner, the puritanical Government of Southern Rhodesia, now Zimbabwe, agreed; they had the statues irreparably mutilated. And so they remain.

None of the Strand's other twentieth-century buildings caused such controversy. In 1924, Rupert D'Oyly Carte, who had taken over at the Savoy, rebuilt the theatre to the designs of Frank Tugwell, with a glamorous interior by Basil Ionides. With its suave lighting effects and rippling patterns, it is now one of the best surviving Art Deco ensembles in London. The hotel had already been extended in 1903, with the building of Savoy Court, faced in a creamy glazed terracotta known as Doulton's Carrara Ware. The entrance from the Strand — now respectable — was given a Jazz Age awning in stainless steel by Sir Howard Robertson in 1929.

Shell Mex, doing well out of the motor age, acquired the old Hotel Cecil in 1930 and built a new headquarters. They kept most of the Strand frontage, however. Behind it, Ernest Joseph of the firm Messrs Joseph created a courtyard leading to an immense office block. On the river front, the skyline is broken by the biggest clock in London. As at the Savoy, the style is Art Deco, if monumental rather than glittering. The clock instantly became famous, being likened, not unreasonably, to the Bakelite clocks often found on suburban mantelpieces. In some quarters it acquired the witty name of Big Benzene. The building, however, is probably better appreciated now than at any time since it was built; certainly authors visiting Penguin Viking, housed within, enjoy the chic detailing, while the vigorous massing of the river front has created a commanding landmark. 'Thoroughly unsubtle,' sniffs Sir Nikolaus Pevsner in The Buildings

'It remains difficult to forgive Colcutt and Hamp's new Adelphi for obliterating its predecessor — Compton Mackenzie likened it to a block of commercial cheese.'

of England volume, but it holds 'its own in London's river front.'

Colcutt and Hamp's new Adelphi office block, finished in 1938, was not to everybody's taste. But Londoners were particularly appalled to see the destruction which preceded it; twenty-four houses by Robert Adam were knocked down in 1936. This affront to the architecture of London followed the demolition of other Georgian landmarks,

FIG 48
*The Shell Mex building. To many people its clock was reminiscent of those that were commonly placed on mantelpieces at the time.*

such as Devonshire House on Piccadilly and Norfolk House in St James's Square, and caused Lord Derwent, Angus Acworth and Robert Byron to form the Georgian Group the next year. It remains difficult to forgive Colcutt and Hamp's new Adelphi for obliterating its predecessor — Compton Mackenzie likened it to a block of commercial cheese. Judged on its own terms, however, the jazzy composition can lift the spirits of those who see it from the terrace. Perhaps to make up for the vandalism of destroying the Adam terrace, the owners allowed money for sculpture. They take the form of carved allegorical figures and relief panels by Gilbert Ledward. There is also a scattering of small panels showing the signs of the zodiac, agriculture and industry, and so on. The effect is jaunty.

Otherwise the Strand did not inspire its landlords to much architectural ambition in the mid-twentieth century. It survived, however, on a human scale, with room for a few oddities from a previous age.

The greatest achievement was not the view to the Strand but to the Thames: the succession of grand masses, from the Adelphi to Brettenham House, on Waterloo Bridge, while not always individually captivating, creates the effect of a monumental parade, softened by the foliage of the gardens before it.

And above all, it survived. The Luftwaffe did its best to wreck it, along with the rest of London. A mine landed near the Savoy; it was also struck by incendiary bombs. The Italian waiters were interned, including, for a time, the popular restaurant manager Loreto Santarelli who had supposedly run a Fascist cell. The Elgin Marbles and other treasures from the British Museum were hidden in the disused tube tunnels at Aldwych Station. American servicemen jitterbugged at the Strand Palace Hotel which became an official establishment for rest and recuperation. Like the rest of England, Northbank emerged into the post-War world grimy, run down and bomb-damaged. But Admiralty Arch, Nelson's Column, the National Gallery, the Hotels and the Law Courts still stood.

'The Greater London Council proposed flattening two thirds of the area between the Strand and Shaftesbury Avenue. The Strand would have become a highway running east.'

What Hitler had failed to achieve the planners then did their best to fulfil. In the 1960s, sleazy and utopian in equal measure, when it came to planning schemes, the Greater London Council, successor to the London County Council, proposed flattening two thirds of the area between the Strand and Shaftesbury Avenue. This would have erased the market. The Strand would have become a highway running east; westward traffic would have come along a parallel artery, several lanes wide, approximately along the line of Maiden Lane. Reader, it nearly happened… but let us distress ourselves no further. In the end it was defeated. From this nadir, architectural ideas could only improve.

The Renaissance of Northbank began in 1978, when Coutts Bank opened their newly remodelled offices at 440 Strand. The architects Frederick Gibberd and Partners had designed the modernist Liverpool Cathedral and planned Harlow New Town. But for Coutts, they did not entirely sweep away the existing building, to replace it by something in the 'spirit of the age' (which invariably meant concrete and glass). Instead they respected the streetscape of the Strand sufficiently to keep the line followed by the façade of the existing building by John Nash, stucco-fronted with a screen of Ionic columns. This was punctured by a glass wall. Behind it, visitors were astonished by the drama of the escalators whisking them up into what felt like the upper echelons of finance. But this spatial excitement co-existed — had indeed been made possible — by the preservation of the façades to either side of the intervention. It was not, perhaps, architecturally polite, but the lesson was nevertheless clear. In the right hands, old buildings and historic neighbourhoods could be fun.

# Chapter Ten
## *The Future*

The river, the road — throughout this study we have seen them to be the defining features of Northbank. It was the Thames that provided the first artery of communication, inspiring the Bishops and more worldly magnates to build palaces along its shore. Parallel to it, the Strand came to provide another essential link between the City of London and royal Westminster. In time, the road, in terms of traffic, got the upper hand. Still an ambiguous area geographically, the no man's land between the Temples of Mammon in the east and those of Fashion in the west, it became the theatre district of the mid-Victorian period, bustling with crowds seeking entertainment after their hard working days, intermingled with prostitutes from the adjacent slums. Those slums were cleared, some to make way for the Law Courts — surely the Gothic Revival's pre-eminent example of street architecture (designed, felicitously, by an architect called Street). The Strand was improved, the Mall created in its present form; and the road became a royal, nay imperial route: symbolism provided the King, as his carriage rolled from the freshly built East front of Buckingham Palace to the creamy new Portland stone of Aldwych, with a mental journey around his Empire. But in all this the river was not forgotten. It provided views. Canaletto understood this, as did, in building the Savoy Hotel, Richard D'Oyly Carte. The need to cleanse the river by building sewers gave Northbank the Victoria Embankment Gardens, as well as a road to relieve the Strand. Whatever the other failings of mid-twentieth century urbanism, it created a bold river front, which can be viewed with pleasure from the South. Unfortunately the river served to guide German bombers into London during the Blitz; but Northbank survived the worst efforts of the Luftwaffe, and even managed to see off the attempt by megalomaniac traffic engineers to turn the Strand into one carriageway of, in effect, a motorway. Gone are the ancient buildings that graced the Strand a century ago; but look carefully — few passers-by, I suspect, have the time to — and its streetscape is peppered with architectural memories of the nineteenth century.

Road and river, flux and change. Both bring people — although they do not tend to linger, being anxious to hurry on to their next destination. It is an area of hotels. Chambers and flats exist for lawyers and other professionals, but Northbank does not have the reputation of being a residential area, although this is changing with the creation of more than 200 apartments opposite the Royal Courts of Justice by Berkeley Homes and a number of other developments being planned. The district is characterised by movement rather than permanence. The one constant is perpetual change.

These themes are reflected in the urban interventions that have led, tentatively, to a Northbank Renaissance in recent decades. Renaissance is a word aptly used of the National Gallery, whose proposed extension, in 1982, was damned by Prince Charles as a 'monstrous carbuncle on the face of a much-loved and elegant friend.' A new competition was held, a donation given by the Sainsbury brothers and — behold — Robert Venturi's new wing

arose to delight museum goers. Visitor numbers soared. Soon the National Portrait Gallery was also remodelled, helped by the generosity of Christopher Ondaatje; one improvement was to create a café-restaurant with a superlative and previously unseen view of Nelson's column.

In the late 1980s, a new station arose above Charing Cross, adding an element of architectural wonder to the daily commute of the passengers using it. British Rail had discovered the value of air rights over its tracks, and using what Farrell calls 'a very innovative and ambitious structural approach' the new development provided nine floors of uninterrupted office space. Architecturally London was given a building of its time: flamboyant, glitzy, far from bashful — but a building to lift the spirits. Its festive air was particularly evident when the lights went on at night. Here was a true piece of river architecture. The self-confidence that it exuded began to spread.

Among Northbank's birds of passage is a student population. Both King's College, London, and the London School of Economics occupy many sites. Their success is giving Northbank, among its other attributes, the character of being an academic quartier. Where students congregate is always life.

They have been joined, in ever greater numbers, by tourists. Nash's vision of Trafalgar

FIG 49
The Garden Bridge:
an artist's impression.

Square as a popular rendezvous and cultural space has been fulfilled. For the course of the last century, Barry's piazza was a traffic island, on which Nelson's column stood proud but unapproachable, except by visitors willing to risk a dash through the oncoming tide of cars and buses. The traffic engineers were adamant: any alteration to the status quo would cause London to seize up. But in 1998, John Prescott announced that a masterplan by Foster and Partners would be implemented. This closed the north side of the square to traffic and restricted movement on the west. The effect was instantaneous. Trafalgar Square opened like a flower. Buskers appeared. Tourists came in their droves. Cafés opened. Events of all kinds are held their under the aegis of the Mayor of London. The geographical centre of London has become its meeting place.

In 2008, the Savoy Hotel was closed for a spectacular restoration. Already Northbank had delighted London with the minimalist, independently minded One Aldwych, created by Gordon Campbell Gray in the old Morning Post building. Off Northumberland Avenue, the Corinthia opened to dazzle the spies who had once haunted a building used by the intelligence services. The hotels of Northbank are seizing the initiative from the West End.

We have seen Somerset House emerge as the eighteenth-century successor to the Lord Protector Somerset's town palace (which he had all too little time to enjoy): Chambers created a palace for civil servants. In 1852-56 it was extended on the west side, along the approach to Waterloo Bridge, by James Pennethorne, an architect whose early career was spent nestled closely under the wing of John Nash. Pennethorne's block was more fully flavoured that Chambers's delicate and well-balanced courtyard, but the profession admired it: the Royal Institute of British Architects awarded Pennethorne a special gold medal in 1857. This wing, in a sign of things to come, was occupied by the Inland Revenue. Their remit included the stamping of newspapers. as John Murray's *Handbook to London* (1856) describes:.

*In rooms two stories below the level of the quadrangle, the mechanical operations are conducted. Legal and commercial stamps are impressed by hand-presses. The name of each newspaper has been inserted, since the reduction of duty in 1836, in the die, in movable type, and by this means a private register is obtained of the stamped circulation of every newspaper in the kingdom. In the basement story are presses moved by steam: some employed in printing medicine-labels, some in printing stamps on country bank-notes; others in stamping the embossed medallion of the Queen on postage envelopes; and others in printing penny and two-penny postage stamps on sheets.*

Above, in realms of light, dwelt the Commissioners, whose rooms corresponded to their status as the overseers of Britain's fiscal probity; the Chairman's salary of £2,500p.a. was the highest in Somerset House. Now, the richly Classical halls through which such luminaries once moved are being thrown open to public uses, in accordance with the mission of the Somerset House Trust. The west entrance will be reopened. Cafés will blossom in the desert of Lancaster Place, leading from Strand to the bridge.

These developments — the extension of the National Gallery, the improvements to Trafalgar Square, the expansion of the academic institutions, Somerset House's new life — lead in one direction. Half a century ago, Northbank's daytime population would have been largely office workers. It now attracts a much more varied mix of people. Perhaps more of them are young. There are tourists, in abundance, from overseas, and what in a previous age would have been called *flâneurs*. Both Londoners and tourists come to visit the National Gallery and Somerset House. Increasingly they come, too, for restaurants. The hotels are world class. They look forward to evenings spent perhaps in some of Northbank's many theatres. Increasingly, Northbank is finding an identity as a place to idle and enjoy life, as well as work.

Soon, a new dimension will be added by the Garden Bridge. Joanna Lumley conceives it as 'a floating paradise garden' suspended above the river Thames. Chancellor George Osborne, who has given £30 million towards it, believes that it will attract 'visitors from across the globe.' Launching itself from Temple Place and touching down beside the National Theatre, the Garden Bridge is set to be opened in 2018. If the result proves to be anything like as popular as the Wobbly (formally Millennium) Bridge opposite St Paul's, it will act as a siphon, sucking the humanity that congregates in Trafalgar Square and Covent Garden along the Strand and across the Thames to the arts institutions of the South Bank. The river, the road — the Garden Bridge is, so to speak, the joyous fulfilment of an historic destiny.

But is either river or road ready for it? Victoria Embankment Gardens has become a popular place of resort for office workers, wanting to rest their eyes on green space. But the river itself is hidden from view. The walk beside it is cut off by the rush of traffic on the Embankment: few people are seen walking there, compared to the crowds in Trafalgar Square. There is little for them to do beyond stroll when they get there. The Strand, despite the rearrangement of the carriageway in recent years, remains a street where it is impossible to linger. The pavements are too narrow for the number of people going down them. Many of those people are in a hurry. Take out a camera and you risk being knocked off your feet. It has always been a bustling thoroughfare but Pepys and Dr Johnson found it possible to spend the time of day here; Strand has, in the intervening centuries, forgotten the art of living gently. The texture of the street is often harsh.

Imagine if it were, at weekends or even permanently, closed to traffic. Imagine if cafés and restaurants could spread their tables in an atmosphere not choked with exhaust. Imagine if people, on the way from Trafalgar Square to the Garden Bridge, stopped here to refresh themselves, or explore the remarkable history of the side streets. The benefit would not only be to holidaymakers. Office and shop workers would find this a more agreeable environment. The character and rents of the area would rise. At present, you cannot lift your eyes to enjoy the architecture of the Strand: some busy person will collide with anyone who tries to. But the physical ambience at street level belies its rich history. It can seem, at times, gritty. So not enough passers-by are beguiled to spend an hour or two in the district; there's too little to delight the eye at street level. But imagine that there were more tables along the Strand, and trouble taken to ensure a better quality of design. Could it once again be Britain's Burse?

Why not?

'Imagine if the Strand were, at weekends or even permanently, closed to traffic. Imagine if cafés and restaurants could spread their tables in an atmosphere not choked with exhaust. Imagine if people, on the way from Trafalgar Square to the Garden Bridge, stopped here to refresh themselves, or explore the remarkable history of the side streets...'

FIG 50
The Strand, bustling

# Image Acknowledgements

COVER IMAGE
*St Paul's* by Jo Bowen
www.jobowen.co.uk

FIG 1
© Northbank BID

FIG 2
Public domain, Yale Center for British Art

FIG 3 (ROMAN BATHS)
© Sam Peach
www.sampeach.com

FIG 4
© The Bulldog Trust

FIG 5
© Richard Croft, CC BY-SA 2.0

FIG 6
© Museum of London

FIG 7
Public domain, Royal Air Force

FIG 8
© Ronnie MacDonald, CC BY 2.0

FIG 9
© Zyllan Fotografía, CC BY 2.0

FIG 10
© Sam Peach

FIG 11
© Queen's Chapel of the Savoy

FIG 12
Public domain, scanned from *Antiquities of Westminster*, John Thomas Smith, 1806

FIG 13
Public domain, downloaded from Wikimedia Commons

FIG 14
© National Portrait Gallery

FIG 15
© Sam Peach

FIG 16
Public domain, Project Gutenberg. From *The Mirror of Literature, Amusement, and Instruction, No. 365*, various authors, 1829

FIG 17
© Doc Searls, CC BY 2.0

FIG 18
© Chris Holifield, CC BY-SA 2.0

FIG 19
© Sam Peach

FIG 20
© Rob Farrow, CC BY-SA 2.0

FIG 21
© Poppet with a Camera, CC BY 2.0

FIG 22
Public domain, Berger Collection

Fig 23
© Sam Peach

Fig 24
Public domain, Metropolitan Museum of Art

Fig 25
© Sam Peach

Fig 26
Public domain, Yale University Art Gallery

Fig 27
© Sam Peach

Fig 28
Public domain, scanned from *The Story of London's Underground*, John Day and John Reed, 1963

Fig 29
© Sam Peach

Fig 30
© Sam Peach

Fig 31
Public domain, scanned from *Cartoon portraits and biographical sketches of men of the day*, Frederick Waddy, 1873

Fig 32
© Andrea Vail, CC BY-ND 2.0

Fig 33
© National Maritime Museum

Fig 34
Public domain, Library of Congress/Detroit Publishing Co

Fig 35
Public domain, downloaded from Wikimedia Commons

Fig 36
© Sam Peach

Fig 37 (ROMANO'S)
Public domain, University of Nevada, Las Vegas

Fig 38 (SIMPSON'S-IN-THE-STRAND)
© Simpson's-in-the-Strand

Fig 39 (FOUNTAIN TAVERN)
© Simon Harriyott, CC BY 2.0

Fig 40 (COAL HOLE)
Public domain, Harvard Theatre Collection

Fig 41
© Corinthia Hotel

Fig 42
© National Portrait Gallery

Fig 43
© Sam Peach

Fig 44
Public domain, LSE Library

Fig 45
© Australian High Commission

Fig 46
© Sam Peach

Fig 47
© Sam Peach

Fig 48
© Sam Peach

Fig 49
© Arup

Fig 50
© Liam Bailey/Northbank BID

*Note: 'CC' codes indicate images licenced under Creative Commons. Visit creativecommons.org for full details.*

# Some Further Reading

DAVID G C ALLAN, *The Adelphi, Past and Present*, 2001

SIR WALTER BESANT and G E MITTON, *The Strand District*, The Fascination of London series, 1903

CHARLES DICKENS jr, 'Strand', in *Dickens's Dictionary of London*, 1882

ROBIN GRIFFITH-JONES and DAVID PARK (ed), *The Temple Church in London, History, Architecture, Art*, 2010

COMPTON MACKENZIE, *The Savoy of London*, 1953

*Survey of London*, vol 18

SIMON THURLEY, *Somerset House: the Palace of England's Queens*, 1551-1692, 2009

W MACQUEEN POPE, *Ghosts and Greasepaint*, 1951

# About Wild Research

Wild Research is the thought-leadership and
publication division of the executive search
business Wild Search. Since 2011 we have
produced a dozen publications on both policy-
related issues and corporate histories.

For further information, please visit:

*www.wildresearch.org.uk*